Stuart Neal was the publisher at the ABC for many years and now works as a consultant publisher for Allen & Unwin. Sharon Guest is a playwright and screenplay writer.

Jessie Mei Mei

A girl from a world where no games are played

Sharon Guest &
Stuart Neal

ALLEN&UNWIN

Some of the names in this book have been changed.

First published in 2010

Allen & Unwin
83 Alexander Street
Crows Nest NSW 2065
Australia
Phone: (61 2) 8425 0100
Fax: (61 2) 9906 2218
Email: info@allenandunwin.com
Web: www.allenandunwin.com

Cataloguing-in-Publication details are available
from the National Library of Australia
www.librariesaustralia.nla.gov.au

ISBN 978 1 74237 104 7

Typeset in 12/16pt Minion by Post Pre-press Group
Printed and bound in Australia by Griffin Press

10 9 8 7 6 5 4 3 2 1

FOREWORD

I have known Stuart Neal for some years now in his publishing role as a patient, attentive listener to the kinds of disorganised, rambling book ideas that we journos come up with from time to time. But when I met his partner Sharon Guest, it was in the context of one of the most harrowing stories I have ever reported, and, as she herself so vividly tells it, much of it was taken up with her own heart-wrenching sobs as she described the appalling predicament she and Stuart had faced in caring for their wonderful child, Jessie Mei Mei.

For years Sharon had wanted a child of her own, but if there's a moral in here, it's one of beware what you wish for! Jessie changed their lives in ways so mundane, and yet so profound, that it's impossible as a reader of this tale not to feel their joy and anguish too. Jessie presented Sharon and Stuart with the biggest challenge of their lives. And in meeting that challenge head-on, they learned how to fight, and how to change the world around them for their daughter's sake. It's a tale of extraordinary pain, frustration and guts, shot through with shafts of lightness and love.

Three years ago Stuart and Sharon were struggling parents colliding with a monolithic, emotionless bureaucracy. That they prevailed is a tribute to their fortitude, patience and ingenuity, and there are lessons here for the bureaucrats who tell families how to live their lives; for those who rush to judgment about the decision Sharon and Stuart felt forced to take; and for those who have no concept of the battles faced by parents who care for children like Jessie.

There's an extraordinary symmetry to Jessie Mei Mei's story. Twice she was abandoned by parents—and twice she was rescued by Stuart and Sharon. Their life together has been exhilarating, heart-breaking, traumatic and uplifting. Together they have transcended a litany of horrors through their love for each other—and through a defiance of authority. From the haunting horror of China's orphanages, to the bone-weary grind and personal tragedy that awaited them back in Australia, it's a story of parental devotion given unquestioningly, of small steps forward and huge setbacks, of rage, despair and final acceptance of the inevitable.

This is a uniquely modern love story, spanning two continents in awkward cultural proximity to each other. At its core is the love of a pure, inspiring child, and the power of the ties that bind us all, the invisible red threads reaching out from Jessie Mei Mei to all of us who read this book.

Quentin McDermott
4 CORNERS reporter

CONTENTS

ACKNOWLEDGMENTS

Special thanks to Paul Berchtold and Margaret Johnston from ADHC—as DADHC is now known—for their care and support during a most difficult time.

And to Cindy Lorenz—one in a million.

EAT AN APPLE AND LIE UPSIDE DOWN

Sharon

Someone commented to me recently that because infertility is more widespread these days, couples find it easier to deal with. Experience tells me that whatever the context, it remains a lonely road where longing and primal instinct overtake you. For me, being unable to have children was an all-consuming, constant torment that at times doubled me over with grief. Not all women feel this way and some choose to bypass children altogether, but for me, as the years passed, desperation grew into fear as my fertile years ebbed with each birthday.

My husband Ed (pseudonym) and I never thought twice that we wouldn't be able to procreate and, in the hubris of youth, I thought it wasn't a matter of *if* but a matter of *when*. Ed, an Australian journalist, had been posted to London and we were having a grand old time, but after two years of trying we were mystified a pregnancy hadn't occurred. We sought help.

1

'Well,' said the smiling, bald-headed specialist peering through his bifocals, his demeanour screaming importance, Cambridge and money. He was immaculately presented, but hanging off his face was a purple-veined, bulbous monkey-like proboscis—a deformity unmistakably symptomatic of too much red wine and way too much scotch. On any other day we would have laughed our heads off. I was 28 when he told us we fell into the 10 per cent of infertile couples diagnosed with *unexplained infertility* and should look to IVF.

'What's he on about,' we shouted over each other in the street outside, making for the nearest pub.

'If there isn't a problem it's bloody good news, isn't it?'

'Bloody idiot,' shouted Ed.

'It's just a matter of time, that's all,' I muttered.

'Course it is,' said Ed, draining half his pint in one go.

When I was 31 we sought medical help.

Years and years of arduous, invasive fertility treatment followed on our return to Australia. It was an unforgiving, emotional roller-coaster and eventually my entire happiness revolved around my fertility cycle. Hopes were raised just to be dashed, over and over; it was a living nightmare as, each month, the inevitable period pains unravelled the few remaining vestiges of hope, little by little.

'Eat an apple while standing on your head,' whispered 'Fang', my toothless mother-in-law, without a hint of a smile. If it wasn't the Billings method it was relaxation, hypnosis, herbal medicine, Chinese faith-healers, positive thinking, retreats, diet—eat yams! Even my own mother was at it: 'Why don't you go to Spain?' she said, as if it was the simplest thing in the world.

'A woman in her 50s has just given birth!', she yelled down the phone from England.

But that was only one part of the assault. It seemed everyone, even strangers, wanted to know why I didn't have children. 'Don't you want them?'; 'I thought you wanted to have a baby?' they would ask while I mumbled and fumbled and squirmed like bait on a hook. So frequently did the question rear its head that once, at a party, someone said something I didn't quite hear and before I could stop myself blurted: 'Why don't I have children?' Then there were the other more hurtful comments: 'I only have to *look* at my husband and I'm pregnant.' Then the oversympathetic: 'Believe me, you don't want children. I often wonder why I bothered.' Of course these were always the same people that waxed lyrical about their kids.

Worse still were the drunken macho comments in the pub that had my husband wriggling like a stuck pig: 'Give her to me, mate, and I'll sort her out'; 'What's up, mate, you're not shooting blanks, are you?'

Wherever I looked, women were cooing over babies. Prams and strollers seemed to be everywhere; baby ads abounded on TV; young family members were having babies. I wanted to scream. When I saw a car with the sign 'BABY ON BOARD', such was my frustration I wanted to ram the sign right up the driver's smug, fecund interior. It was definitely time to get a grip when I found out my little cat was pregnant. Looking at its contented, swelling tummy, I felt a furious rage against the world: 'How can it be so hard—even a bloody cat can do it!'

But eventually, as the years passed, instead of nosey questions about when we would have a child, people fell silent. The furtive, sympathetic stares when a baby was brought near me were unbearable. The silence and sad looks were somehow worse because it meant everyone now felt our situation was hopeless.

When Ed and I met I was a backpacker from England and had just turned 23. He was a glorious man: the type every parent wants for their daughter—the type of man who gave to homeless people in the street or regaled a party through egoless, humble humour. Sadly though, like many men, he could not talk about 'our problem'. I, on the other hand, like most women, got solace through verbalising my emotions. I was much younger too and maybe that had something to do with it. Whatever the reason—in the end—we both knew it was over.

The evening I stood in our empty house filled only with packing boxes, I slid down the wall crying with a despair I'd never known. All my dreams of great love and a family were shattered and gone. My body was racked with spasms and the tears of years and years of grief tumbled into the fur of my little dog, Magnus, who had tentatively come to comfort me. I was 40 years old and after 17 years of marriage faced the future alone.

Part One

CHAPTER 1

ST PATRICK'S DAY

Stuart

There was something in the air as I approached John's East Redfern terrace in Sydney on St Patrick's Day. I felt intuitively my life was about to change and for the first time in years there was a lightness to my step. It was as if the two Celtic streams in my blood—the Scottish and Irish—were in a power play and the leprechauns were winning, dancing magical mischief around my dour, Edinburgh academicism with a cheeky glint in their eyes.

But maybe that's fanciful, for as is often said, hindsight's a wonderful thing. My life took a completely new direction that day, a direction which set me on a path that neither I nor anyone could have imagined.

'C'mon, finish ya beer. It's St Patrick's Day, we're going to party!' I knew what John meant, but I was hopeless with women. I'd had a succession of short failed relationships over the years, including a brief marriage in the middle there somewhere about a decade earlier. Yep, I was a loser when it came to love. All I wanted to do now was chew the fat with John in the safety of his lounge room.

But John got me going, as he always did, and half an hour later we both stormed through the Brendan Behan's swinging doors like cowboys in a western after thirty dusty days on the trail. It was dead as a doornail. Someone in a far corner coughed and an unattended poker machine cleared its throat in the distance.

'It's St Patrick's Day!' John boomed as he moved alongside a chubby, balding loner who was drawing pictures with his index finger in the head of his Kilkenny.

'Eh?' said the barman without a trace of Irish brogue, his eyes fixed on the end of a dog race.

'It's St Patrick's Day,' John roared again. 'Where's the band?'

The barman shrugged his shoulders: 'What d'you want?'

'Guinness!' hollered John, who was out for a good time come hell or highwater. '*Two* Guinnesses. It's St Patrick's Day.'

John told me many believed the site of the Brendan Behan was cursed; maybe even some sort of Aboriginal badland. The pub had been through more name changes than he could recount: the Britannia, the Darlington, the 'something' Arms, the Welcome Hotel, to name just a few.

There was nothing for it but to play pool. As I racked the balls for our second game I saw her: a flash out of the corner of my eye.

'What the hell was that?' I murmured to John, who was half asleep in the wash of my sombre introspection.

'Some sheila just skidded into the bar on her knees,' he said, as if it were the most normal thing in the world.

'My round,' I said, feeling a strong pull towards the source of the flash.

As I approached the bar I saw her again. She was more sprite than woman, asparkle and crackling with energy. Her akubra was tipped back, revealing fine strands of red hair framing a heart-shaped, rosy-cheeked face. Her dazzling green eyes were warm and penetrating yet elusive. I turned to pay . . . where had she gone?

'We're playing doubles,' John announced with glee, indicating that the sprite would partner him.

'Christ,' I thought, 'how did he manage that?'

'Who am *I* supposed to play with?' I challenged fiercely, feeling discarded.

'Hi, I'm Sharon, that's Sue over there. She'll play with you. We need some life in here—what d'you reckon?' the sprite said with a twinkle in her eye as she selected a cue.

I grinned idiotically and returned to the safety of a stool by my new partner, Sad-Faced Sue, who had remained glumly in the corner. John, who had the 'charge full' sign flashing, was suddenly nimble for a big man; dancing around the table on his toes as he moved his glass and belongings to the far end. He was taking possession.

Sharon's accent was English but her language was laced with Australian colloquialisms of an age gone by. Everything about her was delightfully spontaneous; she was like a hundred characters rolled into one and when John finally calmed himself and the two of them leant in together in animated conversation, I could only sit and stare.

She talked to John all night. But every now and then she'd come over to my table. She was quick-witted, perceptive and interested in all around her. But I was neither quick nor a joker like John, and before we exchanged three sentences she'd be gone.

It was four games to nil. I'd been winning all night. But Sharon was tactically very astute and this, coupled with her ferocious desire to win, saw me snookered on every play in the next game. It was Sharon's turn; she had one ball left. It was an impossible shot, snookered just behind the black. Walking around the table, I caught her eye as she examined the angle, and a surge of energy coursed through my body. John and Sue were fixed on the game and as Sharon drained her pint of Guinness, a hushed silence descended as she bent in deep concentration to take her shot. She sent the white off the far cushion and hit her ball with astounding precision, spinning it away from the black straight into the middle pocket. The room erupted but there was still the black to go and Sharon's eyes were on that.

'Time gentlemen and ladies!' yelled the barman with one eye on the dogs. Panic set in. The night was over. How was I going to see this girl again, whom I hadn't even managed to hold in conversation? She was leaning in now, about to take her shot as my mind swirled. Then, as if she'd read my thoughts, she looked up and fixed her eyes on mine. The intensity of her gaze burnt right through me and energy rippled in peristaltic waves as if electrodes had been fastened all over my body. Everything and everyone melted away. With the faintest flicker of a smile, she slowly cast her eyes back on the black and hit it directly into the dead-centre of the far corner pocket. I felt I'd woken from a sleepwalker's trance that stretched back all my adult life and then the moment was gone as the lights were set firmly to full neon glare. 'C'mon! Time gentlemen and ladies, please!'

Sharon came over and shook my hand. For the first time her

eyes were averted and I knew in that moment she'd felt something too. My heart raced. Never before had I asked for a girl's number. I'd always just let fate take its course. If the truth be known, I was hopelessly shy.

'I never give my number out,' she said, 'I'll take yours.' I watched her bounce away. 'Actually, hang on,' she hollered, skidding to a halt just inches away, 'I know I won't phone you so what the hell, take mine.'

'Great shot,' I called as she disappeared into the night.

As custom demands I left it a few days, but when I couldn't stand it any longer, I couldn't find her number. For two weeks I turned the house upside down: I searched the fridge, I partially dismantled the washing machine—I asked a mate who sometimes gave me a lift whether I could search his car.

St Patrick's Day had been so full of magic and for a brief moment I thought fate had something else in store for me—something so special that it penetrated the very core of what life is all about. 'Life never does this, of course,' I told myself, 'not for silly idealists like me, not for anyone but the deluded.' But every morning, as the grey dawn light filtered through the blinds of my bedroom, the sprite's face sparkled and flashed mischievously all around me.

CHAPTER 2

MARRIOTT STREET

Sharon

'Got a dollar?' A smiling, teenage Aboriginal in an oversized T-shirt was parked in front of my trolley. Abruptly swerving I narrowly missed an 80-year-old granny in her miniskirt and high-tailed it into the supermarket.

The Surry Hills shopping centre in East Redfern has always reminded me of the alien bar in *Star Wars*. It's another universe to which a bizarre assortment of beings flock and no-one bats an eyelid. Aboriginals, street kids, gays, transvestites, doctors, architects, radio personalities, actors, writers, deros, drunks and druggies; everyone is accepted and nothing is unusual. There is always something going on. If it isn't a security guard galloping down the street after a thief it's someone fainting from sausage sizzle fumes or an all-out screaming domestic or an alcohol-infused brawl. And there is always a desperate addict pleading for drugs outside the medical centre.

I lived across the road and, having spent most of my previous years in a depressed infertility gloom, embraced this mad world as part of my mad, new life. Night and day the energy was palpable, and the sense of community stronger than any I have ever known. All of us have exhilarating moments in life where we can say 'that's when I came in to my own'—this was such a time for me.

My confidence soared and my phone never stopped ringing. There were parties and invitations by the dozen—but I could not believe that Stuart Neal, the shaggy-haired, dour, bespectacled ABC publisher I'd met in the Brendan Behan on St Patrick's Day who'd seemed so desperately interested had not contacted me! *Not* that I was interested: he'd bored the bloody backside off me. But having just won a grant for a film script the possibility of someone with contacts in ABC drama was worth pursuing. But now the 'monotone mumbler' had spurned me; what the hell was his caper?

After three weeks, curiosity mixed with a dash of indignation got the better of me and I did what I never do—I phoned.

Click. 'You've got through to Stuart Neal. Leave a message if you want to.'

'It's me, Sharon. We met at the Brendan Behan. I'm going there on Tuesday for the pool comp. If you want to come, bring a friend,' I growled.

The following Tuesday Stuart, spruced and nervous, was not only exactly on time. He brought a friend—his retired-barrister dad. But true to form, Stuart was an uphill battle and his slow, considered conversation had my eyes rolling. His father on the other hand lit the room with his hearty laugh, huge personality and wild sense of humour.

'With a dad like that he can't be *that* bad,' I thought. But there seemed to be no light at the end of the tunnel and I had no idea why I kept seeing him again and again.

'What d'you mean this bloke hasn't got a sense of humour?' Shane asked mischievously, slapping Stuart on the back as I opened my front door to let them in. They'd been to a night footy match and were joining me for a drink.

I stared dumbfounded as Shane, oblivious, lurched past me down the corridor towards the fridge.

I had known Shane for years. He was a man who could sell a brush to a bald man and was one of my closest friends, but he was also a motor mouth who blurted whatever came into his head with the subtlety of a souped-up V-8 engine. I should have known better and vowed never, ever to confide in the bugger again.

Stuart was still at the door and I could feel his eyes on my back. 'I didn't say you weren't...' I said, turning. 'I mean... what I said to him was ... um,' I mumbled ashamed. 'Actually, I don't know what to say.'

'I do', said Stuart and with his blue eyes searching my face he bent and whispered so close in my ear his breath tingled: 'Hang in there. There's more to me than what you see.' And with that he was gone, loping down the corridor after Shane, leaving me confused and bewildered. Why wasn't he angry?

As time passed I realised there was indeed far, far more to Stuart. He was different. He would cook as much as me, clean, buy groceries, do the washing. He exhibited no jealousy when I went out, late into the night, with male friends. When I accompanied my single girlfriends to singles clubs he understood. Indeed, sometimes when we couldn't get a taxi, he drove us there—and he could be very, very funny.

Within six months we were living together.

Life is full of surprises. When I first went out with Stuart I didn't think I'd last the night. Even after he moved in I felt the relationship was doomed. His thought was deliberate while mine was rash; my conversation was exuberant and passionate while his was slow and considered. The 'honeymoon' lasted six months and then we had a fight.

'Don't you see,' I yelled at him, 'arguing in public indicates to others you're dissatisfied.' Stuart had made a sarcastic joke at my expense while we dined with two friends and I was furious. 'If you think I can't take criticism well bloody tell me privately but don't ever humiliate me—or YOURSELF—in public ever again!' I shouted knowing—as I'd always known—he wasn't the man for me. 'I won't stand for it, Stuart. A relationship that's full of crap may be good enough for you, but it sure as hell ain't good enough for me!' With that I slammed the bedroom door and lay in bed waiting for him to slam the front one shut, for good.

But the house remained silent.

'Right,' I thought next morning when I saw him on the lounge, 'here we go.' Stuart was looking at me shaking his head but I wasn't about to back down.

'I've been thinking about what you said and what happened last night,' he said purposively.

'Yep, it's on for young and old,' I thought, weighing up which friend I'd stay with while he moved out.

'You're right.'

'Pardon?'

'It was stupid.'

'Pardon?' I said again.

'Public arguments are horrible; I want a better relationship too. It was wrong what I did, I'm sorry.'

'Let's walk the dog,' I said, feeling the need for fresh air and something to defuse the situation.

Some Aboriginals were in the local park under the 'ALCOHOL PROHIBITED' sign having a drink. They'd lit a fire earlier in the day under the tree. The tree was now on fire and the park bench looked about to go up too.

Magnus, my miniature schnauzer, catapulted forward when we turned into a tree-lined street. It was by far the prettiest street in East Redfern. The houses were all renovated, signalling the sweeping gentrification of the suburb. The rich autumnal foliage was uplifting and Stuart tentatively took my hand. I had expected an ongoing argument of justification, where nothing would be resolved, where unspoken bitterness would remain, percolating under the surface, rising again only to fuel another argument until—as happens—all care is eroded, leaving just an empty shell of acrimonious resentment. But once again Stuart had turned my expectation upside down. He had listened, considered—and agreed. I had never met a person who under criticism in the heat of an argument could see when they were wrong. It filled me with deep respect.

It also taught me something about my own inability to take criticism, and I knew from that day on, I would live by Stuart's example. If there was an issue he could voice it; I would listen because it came from a platform of trust. It was a moment that cemented our relationship and as we walked together hand in hand, I knew I'd finally found the type of love I'd been looking for.

It was a wonderful heady time where, with each new day, it became more and more apparent that there was indeed more to Stuart than met the eye. He'd read widely. He was interested in science, history and philosophy, loved music and theatre, played the guitar like no-one I'd ever heard, was always in for a good time and had more friends than anyone I'd ever met. Even down to the hippy bag he carried over his suit jacket, there was always something to surprise me. We watched World Cup football, staying up all night; we played pool, bet on horses, watched boxing fights, always had visitors in our house and energetically discussed every topic under the sun.

And then I got the biggest surprise of all. With hands shaking and my heart pounding, I had to sit down before my legs gave way. Sitting in the bright sunshine that saturated my north-facing lounge, wonder filled my body. I was pregnant.

The pregnancy was into its sixth week when some early morning bleeding sent us rushing to the doctor.

'Everything's as it should be,' the gynaecologist reassured us. 'See that?' He was pointing to a tiny, pulsing light flickering on the ultrasound screen. That tiny heartbeat to this day is the most poignant image I've ever seen. After so long, there it was, my baby blinking back at me, plaintively—I'm yours, look after me. That light looked strong, regular as clockwork and as reliable as a lighthouse. I dared to hope.

But if someone dictates our destiny, they do it with a cruel and heartless sweep because the next day the light went out.

CHAPTER 3

THE JOURNEY BEGINS
Sharon

Six months later I found myself staring at my reflection in the bathroom mirror, trapped by the pointlessness and cruelty of life. How long had I been standing there? I didn't know and didn't care. My face was hard; my eyes milky, unfocused and lost. A huge weight had pinned me down. I couldn't even move my shoulders. Stuart poked his head through the bathroom door. 'Why don't we adopt?' he suggested.

'We're too old,' I mumbled.

'Won't hurt to ask,' he said.

Then we laughed together. 'Have I told you lately . . .' I sang as I playfully pushed him out of the way.

Later that evening I heard Stuart shouting out my name above the din as he scoured the internet. The gays next door were having a dance party; on the other side Mahler symphonies blasted in competition.

'Sharon!' he shouted again, smiling broadly. 'We're not too old!' His face was glowing. 'You can adopt up to the age of 55 in some countries.'

'We could adopt two!' I gasped, amazed.

'We could adopt two, for sure.'

'Maybe we can adopt two together!'

We were now both so excited our conversation was overlapping.

That night we gave our partying neighbours a reason never to turn their music down.

On 29 January 2001 our journey officially began when we lodged our expression of interest with NSW DoCS' international adoption program.

DoCS, now renamed Community Services, is the only organisation in Australia allowed to process international adoptions. Each state may not share exactly the same approach but what they all have in common however, is a frustratingly slow bureaucracy. Thus an interminable five months later we were on our way to our first adoption seminar in Parramatta.

'Ping' went the lift. Taking a deep breath, we walked into the seminar room with just seconds to spare. What struck me immediately was the silence. The room had about twenty couples in it, all sitting stiffly, wearing name badges. Most were around the same age as us—early 40s—apart from one white-haired man, a high-paid executive judging from the cut of his suit, with a wife who could have been his daughter. He looked like he had no interest in adopting a child and was there under sufferance while his wife, like an excited, bouncy puppy, announced to anyone who would listen that they were adopting a Chinese child.

'Good morning everybody,' chirped a tall, excessively

smiling social worker as she shimmied towards the whiteboard. 'This morning I told my 16-year-old son he had the worst traits of both my husband and I.' She was beaming; more than a few people gasped in shock. 'The point is that even if we have the best intentions we will always make mistakes.'

'I can't imagine making that one,' Stuart mumbled as I elbowed his ribs, fearing we would be blacklisted as renegades.

'If you've been abused the tendency is to repeat it,' she continued.

'And what about the rest of us!' muttered Stuart, shifting in his seat. I squeezed his hand tightly to silence him, but I too felt rather dismayed. Knowing first-hand how throwaway, unthinking lines can crush a child, I was certain I'd never repeat that pattern.

'Pretty brave thing to say,' whispered a woman to her husband who was sitting next to us.

'Unforgivable!' he replied.

'Who are these lunatics?' hissed Stuart, who I'd rarely seen so worked up.

We were bombarded with theories on loss and grief; how a child feels when they have lost their mother and what a wrench it is when they are taken from the orphanage and placed with strangers. We heard how children are alarmed by the different look, smell and sound of their new adoptive family; about dislocation, problems with bonding, the need to keep their name and heritage.

It was all important information, but I couldn't help thinking: what about the good things?

In the afternoon they wheeled in a young woman who'd fallen pregnant at 18. The father was not interested and she felt compelled to adopt her child out. She'd never lost touch with her child and had a lovely, inclusive relationship with the adoptive family. The room was respectfully silent. We were saddened by her loss and charmed by her goodness.

But by the time she was into her second hour I was weary of her story. The detail was excruciating. Every phone call she'd received, every photograph she'd ever taken, even every meal she'd had with her child was described down to the last crumb. Abruptly the young woman got to her feet and the grateful crowd spontaneously applauded; finally it was over. She held up an arm in thanks, riffled through her bag with the other, plucked out a wad of paper and resumed her seat. One by one she walked us through every pre-school pencil scratch, glue splotch and glitter splash, oblivious to the groans of her captive audience.

Unlike the rest of us this young woman could have her own children. Indeed she could have lots of them. She was there to show us what the 'birth mother' in China would be going through, so that we could empathise with her plight as well as that of the child. She was there to give us a complete understanding. But this lesson had been absorbed three and a half hours earlier and the room by now was as restless as a sack of snakes. The white-haired man was steadfastly gazing out the window, eyes glassy and face taut, as if any minute now he would smash the window and throw himself out. Inwardly I was screaming: 'JUST GIVE ME A BLOODY CHILD!!!'

Ten months after lodging our initial expression of interest we found ourselves once more heading towards Parramatta for the second seminar, 'Adopting an Older Child'. The snail pace was getting to me.

'I don't believe we'll ever get a child,' I said to Stuart as we held hands walking up the street.

'Yes we will,' he said without hesitation. The first seminar had left me traumatised, in fear of knock-back, but Stuart was a pragmatist. 'It's a process, Sharon: play the game, put up with it, on to the next.'

The room was abuzz with people whispering excitedly, all knowing they were edging a little closer to getting a child. 'Any questions?'

A woman in her mid 40s, sitting cross-legged on the seat in front of me, shot her hand up. She'd tried for many years to have her own child. She wanted to 'share' how painful her infertility had been and soon her words were interlaced with sobs. Her high-pitched voice was punctuated with unbalanced shrieks of laughter; she was a fast talker and her frenetic lurches betrayed serious instability. I wanted to whisper gently, 'might be an idea to stop'. I wanted to tell her she was coming over as quite mad and that while I understood the effects of infertility, DoCS might not. But she was not alone. It became apparent that many had freshly endured this bitter disappointment and their despair hung in the room like a shroud.

'You'll all get the baby you want,' said the social worker with a sympathetic smile.

I don't know why I felt so insulted but I did. Perhaps I was oversensitive, but it felt like she was saying, 'There, there, all you poor pathetic desperate middle-aged losers sitting out there— you'll all get your little baby.'

'Today you will hear first-hand the problems you could encounter when adopting an older child,' said another social worker. 'We have asked two couples and a single parent to share their experiences. You will also get to see some of the adopted children.' At this, the room lurched forward in excited antici-pation. Even though you endure these seminars there is an underlying feeling it won't really result in a child. Now we were all to see that it did, and it was thrilling.

The little girl from Colombia was about four years old. We sat spellbound; no-one could take their eyes off her as she drew quietly on the whiteboard. 'When we picked her up,' said the mother smiling at her husband sitting silently beside her, 'the first thing I thought was: "God, she's ugly".' The little girl had no English and drew on, oblivious. People shifted in their seats, averting their eyes. There was no doubting it: she didn't really look like a child—more like a stocky, middle-aged midget. Her skin was dark and her chubby, round face resembled a football decorated with thick, coarse black jutting curls.

'But she's gorgeous!' shouted the 'mad woman' in front of me to a dumb-struck room. The amiable mother laughed and finally the room smiled—no-one could doubt the love in that mother's eyes.

'Okay, we get it,' Stuart murmured. 'Don't expect to get a cute baby doll.'

Still smiling at her husband, the woman continued: 'I was so excited to pick up my second daughter. In the photo we got she was just a baby. When we picked her up I phoned home immediately. "Mum," I said, "you won't believe it, this one is even uglier!"' The room erupted hysterically. This woman's refreshing candour in a world full of pretence and political correctness had surprised and warmed us all.

Another couple was introduced. Only the mother spoke. They sat apart and neither looked at the other throughout. After adopting a little boy they were surprised that their second allocation was a five-year-old girl.

'She's caused a rift between us,' said the woman avoiding her husband's eyes, which was easy as he never took his off the floor. 'She immediately bonded with my husband and made it clear she was daddy's little girl. She openly rejects me. She's very manipulative and plays us against each other and is spiteful and jealous of her little brother. It's been two years now. I try but I don't know if I will ever love her; I'm not even sure I like her.'

She paused and all was silent but for the dull thrum of my pounding heart. My relationship with Stuart was so strong, but in the back of my mind this prospect haunted me. What if a child came between us? The parents looked wrecked and forlorn. Their world had been poisoned. The seduction of adoption is the seduction of love, and only one in that family was nourished.

Next was a single mother. 'I adopted a healthy little baby girl,' she said as her beautiful Ethiopian daughter looked at a book. 'I only found out a few months ago that she's totally deaf; a product of malnourishment . . .' She paused and gulped for air. 'She's already been through so much . . . it's so hard.' The woman looked worn-out and defeated as her words echoed painfully in the room, and our hearts went out to her.

After lunch we were split into small groups. Standing around awkwardly with the DoCS social worker looking on, we discussed parenting an older child. But the moment the DoCS worker moved away, fearful, furtive whispers came flying from all directions: 'When the social worker visits, tell them what they want to hear'; 'Don't disagree with them'; 'We're all being assessed right now'; 'Some people have had their cupboards inspected'; '*Always* tell them you're going to keep the Chinese name'; 'Buy all the books on sale'.

At the end of the day came a Q&A session. Keeping the children's cultural identity is vital, we'd heard, and the first step is to keep their Chinese names. But I had a question: 'I have worked part-time for several years now as an International Student Coordinator at Randwick TAFE and it's curious that almost all my students adopt an English first name, especially Asians. They like to fit in, and having a name like Chang Bum, as some of them do, can make them feel . . .'

Bang! I was instantly denounced as a heretic and for the rest of the session I sat in a cold sweat, fear-fuelled adrenaline coursing through my body. Suddenly I was a little girl again, back in the classroom, awaiting my punishment. What had I done? Had I just stopped the process there and then? I had questioned their orthodoxy and been swatted away like a fly. I couldn't understand how the issue couldn't even be discussed.

From that point on there was a stiff obedience in the group. Even the 'mad woman' remained silent, and only questions requiring further information on the theories we'd heard were posed. As we left, Stuart bought every book on display.

A lot of information from the seminars, however, was invaluable: children from orphanage backgrounds are denied the nurturing that babies get from the moment of birth—the eye contact, the rocking, the clucking and the touch. Consequently these children are well behind their milestones in age development. They need to be taken back to that missed baby stage; to be rocked, tickled and kissed like babies.

Other aspects such as making books of the child's own story, taking photos of the place of abandonment, indeed everything you come across, to give the child some sense of their history, are also important. So is openly talking about adoption from the start with the child and being honest at all times.

But the tone of the seminars bothered us from the outset. The picture wasn't balanced. We were told only to expect problems. There was no suggestion a child may adjust well; no mention that being placed in a loving family after months or years of tough deprivation may see a child bloom and experience joy for the first time. They might as well have said, 'Why are you doing this to yourself?'

Sadly, many potentially wonderful parents dropped out that day.

In the car driving home we were both quiet. Eventually I said: 'It could have all the problems in the world, it could be a gherkin for all I care. And actually, it's good it's probably not going to be a baby because at least it won't be intellectually disabled.'

My sister had been intellectually disabled. No-one really knew what was wrong with her. She was simply 'retarded' as they called it back then and would need my parent's assistance her whole life. She was five years older than me and her condition put enormous strain on our family. Yes, I knew that whatever problems a child had, nothing was as bad as a mind you couldn't reason with.

'That's right,' Stuart said. 'And whatever the trauma, you and I will sort it out.'

CHAPTER 4

THE DEAD TEA BAG AND NO GARAGE

Stuart

In our formal adoption application we'd been asked to write our individual life stories. We loved this bit. You just can't beat writing about yourself. We both wrote with honesty and passion about our past and went on for pages and pages. I talked about the lively social life of my parents and how they were continually entertaining, sometimes with parties of Gatsby-esque proportions. I also described myself as an introvert who often likes to spend time by myself. Big mistake, but more on this later.

Sharon described her working-class Irish parents and an early life wandering from one RAF base to the next—from Germany to Hong Kong to England. She also talked about her parents' unhappy marriage and how moody and black her father could be. Another big mistake.

By February 2002, 13 months had passed since our initial

expression of interest, but for the first time we felt we were actually about to start the process of adopting a child. The seminars were over and we'd graduated to the next stage—a series of interviews with a social worker, Robyn (pseudonym).

Another two months passed before our first interview. Looking back it's hard to see why we were so apprehensive. 'Nobody gets knocked back,' we'd been told by those who'd been through the mill already. 'Not unless they have a criminal record or a major health problem.' But it didn't seem that easy back then: they were sending out a lone stranger to sit in judgment on us. There was no other way you could look at it and it just didn't seem right.

We started to prepare. We went over our seminar notes and tried to anticipate the questions we might be asked. Sharon in particular was anxious. 'Don't go on and on like you do,' she warned. 'And for goodness sake spruce yourself up a bit.' We scoured the house from top to bottom, burnt incense in the toilet and overdosed on vanilla wipe in the kitchen. We upgraded the sweet biscuits and stocked up with every possible variety of coffee and tea. Potentially embarrassing objects such as our red wine rack were hidden from view, and kitsch we couldn't abide—mostly gifts from well-meaning friends and family— was resurrected in a pathetic effort to look 'normal'.

But our inner confidence was sustained by the absolute bond between us: a wonderful balance of music, literature, love and communication. There was carefree merriment, genuine care and intellectualism in the world we'd created for ourselves; everyone was welcome, everyone's point of view counted, underdogs were nurtured and included, but nothing surpassed the care we had for each other. What could go wrong? We had an inner confidence too of our ability to nurture and love a child together. When two street kids gravitated to our house at Christmas it was clear what succour they got that day. We did this together. We did everything together.

On 11 April 2002 the big day came and the scrubbed-out house was neat as a pin. It looked like it was on the market, ready for inspection. All that was missing was the sandwich board out the front and the immaculately suited agent by the open door, clipboard in hand. Robyn arrived in a swish of long skirts. She wasn't used to the city and was overwhelmed and anxious about parking her car outside on a street in Redfern. Once we assured her that all would be fine and that I'd check on her car at regular intervals she became calm.

Then, to her credit, she did her best to put us at ease. She was empathy personified, nodding and smiling. She was softly spoken and a stroker. The smallest remark was met with a cornucopia of care. When I asked, 'Could you pass the sugar please?' she looked at me with eyes that said, 'I know what it's like. It's really hard on you to have the sugar out of reach but together we can work through this problem.'

Before the interview began Sharon had been keen to explore the possibility of adopting from Africa. 'China's your best option,' said Robyn, nonplussed. We hadn't discussed the choice of country with anyone until now and Sharon wanted to know about all the different programs and pressed further. 'I don't have details of the various programs, you'll have to ask DoCS,' Robyn said finally.

'Okay,' I said, 'tea or coffee?' wondering all the while how China could be our best option if she knew nothing about any of the programs.

As I handed out the tea, including a herbal one for Robyn

which she had brought herself, I said cheerily, 'So how do we go about this?'

'Right . . . right . . . well . . . well, goodness, where shall we start?' Robyn asked, scanning her list of questions, still a little flustered by Sharon's earlier persistence.

'Why not start from the top,' I suggested.

'Yes, yes,' she said with a nervous laugh. 'Have either of you been sexually abused?'

'Err . . . no,' I said.

Sharon, who looked like she might burst out laughing, shook her head.

'That's good,' said Robyn, marking her paper. 'Now let me see. Ah, here we are. Why do you want to have children?'

And so it went and we breathed a huge sigh of relief. The answers they wanted to hear were easy to guess. 'Why did we want to have children?' We knew what to say from the seminars. 'We have a wonderful, beautiful, strong relationship which is the envy of our friends and associates. But we want to share our love for each other with children to make our lives complete. We want to be a family.' Robyn beamed as she took notes. 'Top answer,' she seemed to be thinking as she smiled broadly, but I suspected there might be some cunning behind that peaceful, happy exterior.

Sharon made Robyn a cup of tea while I checked on Robyn's car parked on the street.

'No, no, no! Don't throw it out!' Robyn panicked, pointing to her BYO herbal tea bag, which Sharon was dangling above the kitchen tidy. 'I prefer to recycle,' she said.

'Car's still fine,' I said, resuming at the table. 'Did I miss anything?'

'In your family, how was self-esteem developed?' Robyn

read carefully, her doleful eyes radiating sympathy, anticipating the worst.

'It's in the life story,' I said.

'Yes, well, I haven't read it all yet.'

'It's not very long,' I replied.

'Um . . .'

'Look, I have it here . . . I'll read it to you,' I said. Robyn was sweet and actually very insightful when it came to issues of early child development, but it was galling that DoCS would send such a fish out of water to sit in judgment on us. Alas, tolerance has never been my strong suit.

When it was Sharon's turn she just said more simply, 'My parents were very encouraging, especially my mother. She sang my praises every day.'

'In what way?' probed Robyn, penetratingly.

'In every way,' Sharon replied.

Again Robyn beamed. Sharon was much more efficient than I was. Don't worry about the complexities, don't try and be precise about it, don't even worry about the truth if it comes to that, just tell them what they want to hear.

At the end of the interview Robyn had a question just for me. 'Do you think your parenting experience with Jo, your teenage daughter, will be helpful when it comes to the next child?'

'Yes,' I said with new-found economy. Satisfied with this answer Robyn made a note, packed up her belongings and extended a limp hand in farewell.

Sharon's ageing, albino devon rex, Pugsley, was at the window whingeing for food. Dried green snot was smeared around his cancerous snout. He wasn't the full quid, this cat. For days on end he slept on top of the toilet cistern, which could only be flushed by gently depressing his spine. No matter what you tried he was always filthy moments later, his coat full of grit, and he had the foulest breath of any creature I'd encountered. Sharon went to her dying pet. She scratched him under the chin and looked him over from head to tail for a long time before splintering some freshly cooked chicken breast for him.

The face-to-face process with Robyn continued for the next four months or so. On her second visit we got better at it. We kept it simple. We started to have a little fun too, albeit gently. When Robyn quizzed me about China I got carried away, forgetting Sharon's warning a month previous. I launched into a potted history of the dynasties and the technologies the Chinese had invented. I moved on to the advent of Mao and the Cultural Revolution. Finally I spoke whimsically of the curious, contemporary mix of Communism and capitalism that is present-day China.

'It's great you know so much about it,' she said encouragingly. 'What clothes do you think you'll take when you travel?'

'When are we travelling?'

'Let's see … mmm … maybe March next year,' she said optimistically.

'It's a big place, where are we going?'

'Doesn't matter, what do you think you'll take if it's say, late summer/early autumn?'

'But China's in the northern hemisphere.' Poor Robyn: it had been such an innocent question but my pedantry reared its head irrepressibly.

'What difference does that make?' she continued.

'The tropics aside, it'll either be late winter or early spring.'

'Really? What happens in the tropics?'

'It's either wet or dry but it's always hot.'

'Goodness.'

Robyn went back to her list of questions: 'Do you plan to bring aspects of Chinese culture into your lives and the life of your adopted child?' Our answers proudly featured in her report:

> Mr Neal has published books about the history of China and genuinely believes it to be one of the most sophisticated culture (sic) in the world and looks forward to building a cultural history with his adoptive child.

But it was Sharon who really let loose:

> When the child is older Ms Guest intends to have a Chinese student live with the family periodically. They intend to expose their child to Chinese cultural events, food, music, art, religion and language classes in Mandarin/Cantonese . . . The applicants intend to learn the language of their adopted child . . .

Robyn's last question of the second interview was, 'Have you ever taken drugs?' I kicked off and confessed trying dope at uni, but Sharon, who was known as the 'bong queen' in her uni days, vehemently said she'd never tried drugs and never would with such conviction that even I believed her. She went on to decry the poisons in everyday analgesics like aspirin and codeine. Once again Robyn beamed, but as soon as she left Sharon washed down two Nurofen Plus with a neat scotch.

Apparently there were serious deficiencies with our house that had to be addressed. 'Two bedrooms simply won't do,' Robyn had insisted. The fact that one was currently used just as an office made no difference. But in the end Robyn's most strident criticism focused on our lack of a garage. She just couldn't get her head around this at all. For our part, we couldn't for the life of us see what she was on about.

Robyn's smile returned when we placed the house on the market and promised to move into a four-bedroom house in the suburbs with a triple garage.

The vet said he could operate on Pugsley's face, cut half of it away, and prolong his life by ten weeks or so.

'We have to put him down,' Sharon said, heaving with sobs.

'The vet's keen to do the operation,' I said.

'How will Pugsley benefit from that?' Sharon cried, angrily. 'The vet's a bloody idiot!'

'Or a greedy bastard,' I said.

The day Pugsley was put down Sharon cried all afternoon. It's a shame DoCS wasn't there. They would have seen the grief of a woman who loved and cared deeply. They would have seen a born nurturer. And if they'd had any sense, they would have approved us there and then.

Sharon had really been enjoying talking about herself to Robyn in dribs and drabs, but when she had her one-on-one with Robyn in May she thought all her Christmases had come at once. She loved it. She went for broke and didn't hold back on anything. After two hours she still had plenty to say and marvelled that Robyn seemed to be listening as attentively as ever. 'She must be bored with this by now,' thought Sharon. 'How can she stand it? What the hell. Give me more!' But we both knew Robyn was genuinely interested in everything we had to say. And by now I knew she didn't have a cunning bone in her body. She wasn't hoping we would trip ourselves up—she really cared.

From what I gather Sharon spent a great deal of time

explaining how the inadequacies of her own parents shaped her views on parenting. She was not going to repeat the mistakes they made, particularly those of her father, who was often deeply unhappy, surly and cold. She was determined that this negative in her past would become a positive for the prospective child. Fearing Robyn was trapped in orthodox 'Freud 101', Sharon explained herself every which way. She had moved on from her childhood hurts and her experience was instructive; self-esteem was the least of her problems and she was nothing like her father.

Sadly Sharon's fears were realised when Robyn wrote in her report:

> She [Sharon] has insight into the effects of her upbringing, accepts her parents with their good and bad points. When she becomes a parent herself, she may need to work through those parenting issues again.

Two weeks later I was due for my own one-on-one session. Sharon didn't beat around the bush as she went out the front door: 'If you say anything bad about me, I'll kill you!' The doorbell rang and I was strangely nervous. Robyn greeted me like a close friend at a loved one's funeral. She oozed sympathy before we even started. I'll never forget the way she cupped my forearm with one hand and gently stroked its hairy top with the other.

After extricating myself I concentrated on how living with Sharon had turned my life upside down. I talked endlessly about how happy I was to be bathing in the splendour of such great love. And for once in this charade, I meant every word.

But Robyn's thoughts drifted in one particular direction: 'How is your sex life with Sharon?'

'Terrific,' I said, taken aback.

'Mmmm.'

'It's great. Never been better.'

'Mmmm. Sometimes things go a little sour after there've been fertility problems. How often do you have sex?'

Again, I couldn't help myself: 'We have sex all the time, every morning, every night, sometimes in the middle of the day . . .'

'Well, what did she ask?' Sharon demanded on her return.

'Oh, I love you so much!' I effused. I wrapped my arms around her, lifted her off the floor in a giant bear hug, teetered and crashed to the floor with Sharon writhing on top of me, laughing her head off. In that moment neither of us had a care in the world.

Finally the interviews were over and Robyn wrote her report. It was riddled with myriad errors but we decided to only correct the biggest issues of fact. After all, it was now almost two years since we'd first contacted DoCS and we were desperate to mini-mise further delay. But we couldn't let it go that for a couple of pages in the middle of the report the names of two complete strangers were used instead of ours. We sent our corrections back within a day; our feelings towards Robyn soured when we learnt she did not file the report until three months later.

All in all, the interview process took nearly eight months. The report was very positive and we were confident—but Inter-national DoCS was less convinced and our file languished in someone's in-tray. Eventually I was called in on the grounds that I may repeat the exuberant drinking of my father—a sup-plementary report on this danger would have to be made. A further two months passed and still we had heard nothing; it was now December. Sharon was in a state of high anxiety. We'd got married to satisfy the adoption criteria and complied with all the rules: what was the hold-up? I rang them and firmly insisted on an explanation. The next day a highly embarrassed junior clerk rang me at work.

'I think I know what you're going to say but I've been asked to contact you to clear up one last point.'

'Shoot,' I said.

'How do you ... um ... how do you think that you being introverted ... um ... will affect your ability to parent your adoptive child?'

'Are you kidding?'

'I've been told to ask you this. Sorry.'

I was fuming, but I couldn't take it out on the messenger.

'Okay. Let's try this. Fifty per cent of people are introverted. They get renewal from time alone as opposed to extroverts who recharge themselves through community. You might as well ask an extrovert how they'll cope without lots of people milling around when they're alone with the baby. Anyway, to think that half the population might be disqualified from adopting a child on this basis is patently ludicrous. How does that sound?'

'That's really good. Thank you.'

On 29 January 2003, International DoCS declared us 'eligible and suitable' to adopt a child from China—subject to more police and health checks and the payment of a pile of money. It had been two years to the day since their 'process' began. And what was this process? Two one-day seminars in the first year, and five interviews in the second year. Seven days contact in two years.

CHAPTER 5

RED THREADS OF DESTINY

Sharon

When we were finally approved to adopt, Stuart said 'That's it, we're home and dried,' and put his feet up and relaxed. But after trying to have a child for 14 years and falling at the final hurdle more times than I could bear to remember, my guard was well and truly up. 'What can go wrong now?' Stuart pleaded. I just didn't believe any of it.

Being Irish by blood, my childhood had been suffused with fantastic stories. It was a magical whirl of leprechauns, fairies and spirits where superstitions impregnated every moment. There was a lot to be careful about—from never putting shoes on the table or umbrellas up inside, to never letting a bird fly into the house because it meant death. There were literally hundreds of things to be wary of and curiously, they were about the only things that were ever taken seriously.

Perhaps, along the way, my old Irish mother's prophetic

assessment had taken root in my subconscious and sprouted into an almighty bloodsucker of a tree. 'It's not your destiny to have children, Sharon,' she'd say in her thick brogue. 'God has another path for you. You have the gift.' At this, she would peer into my eyes with a knowing look.

The 'gift', according to Irish lore, is only bestowed on those born at night. Such children have a sixth sense and are able to see spirits and other unworldly things. 'And you were born at midnight,' she'd say, with her deep throaty voice taking on an eerie quality as she looked at me, nodding. But the fact that neither of my parents knew what day I was born made me very distrustful of her midnight story. 'I'm sorry,' said the manager of the club I wanted to book for my 18th birthday. 'According to your birth certificate you're not 18 until the day after.' This was how I found out my birthday had been celebrated for 17 years on the wrong date. 'The hospital got it wrong. What's the big deal anyway?' dismissed my mother. '*My* father didn't even know what year I was born.'

To take my mother's prophecy seriously was absurd. Nevertheless I was unable to shake my Irish heritage and now believed it wasn't my destiny to have children. Stuart, in an effort to jolly my spirits, pointed out we'd been approved. 'It isn't a matter of *if* but a matter of *when*,' he said time and time again. But this just made things worse. I remembered using the same phrase myself, long ago, and I wasn't going to make that mistake again.

The Irish always believe things come in threes—be it good luck, bad luck or death. So, you wouldn't read about it! The day we moved into our new house was the same day our file was sent to China. It was also the day that SARS broke out and inter-country adoption was frozen—indefinitely. Even Stuart was shaken when it happened.

'What did I tell you?' I wailed through tears. I was ready to switch country programs, go overseas, look at fostering, but Stuart, dependable as ever, recovered quickly and was pragmatic and optimistic: 'We wait it out, it will pass, don't worry, Sharon. Believe *me*—not that Irish nonsense!'

In the end Stuart proved to be right and after a few months the SARS scare was over. We were on the move again and about to enter the world of 'Batch 13'.

When you adopt from China you don't collect your child alone, you go in a group with other adoptive parents. Our group was the 13th batch to adopt from China. Thirteen of course to the Irish is a very unlucky number—but I refrained from pointing this out to Stuart, who'd had enough of my emotionally strung-out superstitions.

'What do they want to meet up for?' I said, surveying the friendly three-line email from a member of Batch 13 as one might an unfavourable tax return. 'We're adopting a baby, we're not adopting friends!' I could see by Stuart's face that the noise of my mind ticking over was deafening him, so I just stared at the piece of paper in my hands. An email from someone travelling with us to China meant it was really going to happen. Soon, some small child—age, gender, region unknown—would enter our world and become part of our lives forever. I was suddenly terrified. Like a roller-coaster ride, we were commencing the slow, ominous pull to the top. Soon we would be on a high-speed, spine-tingling, free-fall into the unknown.

I managed to compose a friendly response to the email of 'let's talk closer to the time', and relaxed now I'd put things off. After the setback of SARS we had no idea how long the wait would be and we fell into a strange world where every now and then we would abruptly remember that we were actually adopting a child. I seemed to walk around in a daze wondering whether it would ever happen, sometimes wondering how it came to pass because it all started so long ago. And always in the back of my mind I was waiting for someone to tell me it would never be.

Embedded in the world of international adoption is a matrix of hundreds of websites where information and gossip is exchanged daily. The Rumour Queen's identity is unknown, but when it comes to China she is the hub of it all. Her site (http://chinaadopttalk.com) provides a feast of information about Chinese adoption, expected time frames and photos of babies adopted. Many countries around the world—from Spain to Scandinavia, from the Americas to Australia—link in to share and obtain information. Indeed, The Rumour Queen often knows what's going on well before DoCS and other agencies do.

Towards the end of 2003 there was suddenly an avalanche of emails from two members of Batch 13 who were becoming very excited. According to The Rumour Queen, the Chinese were tearing into the backlog with gusto and our time was quickly approaching. But having never yet met anyone in Batch 13, this frenzied flood of correspondence made me wary. 'A picnic!' I yelled derisively to Stuart. 'What's wrong with meeting in the pub? I told you these weren't my sort of people!'

Truth be known I had my head firmly in the sand.

It was 4 p.m. on Thursday 22 January, 2004 and we'd just returned from the Tamworth Country Music Festival. After a relative silence from Batch 13 members, the emails had been flying all day and every time I looked at my computer there were more. Word had spread from Spain that allocations were arriving, and for some reason one group member was convinced Batch 13 would be part of it.

I ignored them. I was working on a TV script for the ABC and needed time to complete it. I wasn't ready to start the adoption process at all now. It was suddenly tumbling in far too fast.

The phone rang. I thought it was Stuart and rushed to pick it up, always glad to hear his voice. It was DoCS. 'Is that Sharon Guest?'

What did he want; was something wrong? 'Here we go,' I thought, 'one more hold-up; one more disappointment, one more step towards the fulfilment of my mother's prophecy.'

'Congratulations,' he said. 'You have been allocated a baby girl from Guangxi.'

My heart stopped, missed a beat and then was pounding so hard I could almost feel ringing in my ears. 'She's 18 months old; her name is Yang Jia-Mei. I don't have a lot of details. She was very sick and underweight at birth,' and then hurrying on, 'but she's absolutely fine now.' My heart nearly seized when he said, 'I'm emailing the photo now.'

It was a miraculous moment: from another part of the world, a child born to others with no connection was suddenly placed with us. The Chinese call it 'the red threads of destiny'. Steeped in folklore like the Irish, the Chinese believe that when a child is born, invisible red threads spring from the infant's body and connect it to all those who will be important in that child's life. If the threads get tangled, they will never get lost but will eventually connect to those the child is destined to meet.

With trembling hands I put the kettle on, but who was I kidding? I had to look now. So as the kettle gurgled and started to steam I ascended the stairs to my study with the deliberate care of an army scout, slowly, one at a time, as if some monster lay in wait on the landing. At the top I took a deep breath, and then another.

Myriad images flashed through my mind and I marvelled that the little girl I was about to see had been chosen for me far, far away in Beijing. What made them see that Yang Jia-Mei was the one for us? I visualised the official in the 'matching room' with photos of us pinned next to a computer screen displaying countless images of Chinese children. The official had access to our likes, dislikes, personalities, professions, hobbies and talents, but would not need them—just the photos, as she drew on some sixth sense that remains a total mystery to us in the West.

I stood at the computer and willed my hands into action. My body tingled all over as my fingers fumbled on the keys. The computer took an eternity to crank up. Impatiently I pounded the keyboard, trying to hurry it up, but only made matters worse. Finally I zeroed in on the email attachment that contained the photo of our new baby daughter, Jia-Mei (pronounced by us as 'Zha-May', as in Zha Zha Gabor). It was a lovely name and I vowed never to change it.

I sat down, anxious yet thrilled and bristling with antici-pation. The cursor hovered over the attachment—click! My breathing was fast and my chest was heaving as her picture slowly materialised into a small child with black tufts of hair in a baby bouncer. She was bundled into so many layers of clothes she reminded me of a mini Michelin Man.

'They've got to be bloody joking!' I said aloud in horror as the kettle screamed its high-pitched wail downstairs.

Jia-Mei was around nine months old when the photo was taken. 'She's not that bad,' said Stuart, staring at the computer a couple of hours later. 'Look at her long fingers. She'll be a great piano player.' 'That's my man,' I thought: gently placating my fears, but completely missing my point. He saw potential for music. I saw something else and it made me uneasy. But for Stuart, a natural musician, nurtured on classical music and jazz as a child, the moment he saw little Jia-Mei's 'piano fingers' she was 'his girl'.

'It's in the eyes,' I said, 'something in the eyes.' Jia-Mei wasn't looking at the camera, instead she was turned to the side with her mouth open, fat cheeks squashed up against her white Michelin Man jacket. Thick dark eyebrows and a puffy face; she was looking away and she looked hard. Others, including Stuart, thought she was cute. It wasn't external looks I was talking about. It was something deep in her eyes that unnerved me.

What do you do in a situation like this? You can't say: 'No, I don't want that one.' But when I saw all the other children who'd been allocated in our batch and their smiling open faces, my heart ached and I wished I could.

It's a surreal experience receiving a photograph of a child who will then be with you for the rest of your life. A child you know nothing of who is chosen for you by someone else. Some people in our batch fell in love with their photos immediately. I couldn't understand that. Love for me takes time to grow; it always has. When it does become love it is strong, impenetrable, a living being in itself. As I looked at the photo over and over I had no idea of the enormous love I would come to feel for this little urchin: Yang Jia-Mei.

Now it was really on! Batch 13 was in overdrive. If hysteria had reigned before, the frenzy to get organised and over to China as soon as humanly possible was nothing short of madness. And as I was battling with a script deadline that was drowning me, it fell to Stuart to get things organised.

Roberta Clapton (pseudonym) had become the de facto leader of our group, entirely through the power of her emails. There was nothing she hadn't researched. She also set deadlines for all our paperwork, issued homework assignments and basically kept SS Batch 13 on course. She was determined to ensure that nothing, absolutely nothing, got in her way as she focused on the surest path to her new baby.

Her indefatigable help proved invaluable. Stuart first met Roberta at the Department of Immigration at Parramatta, where she stood by waiting for him to turn up like a sentry guarding the fort. Although they'd never met she found him in a trice. For hours she'd held his place in the queue by refreshing the numbered tickets over and over, and when he finally arrived she stood tall at the counter like Brunhild challenging all who might deny him clear and swift passage.

They were there to secure special visas for our children to enter Australia indefinitely after they were adopted. Roberta had completed her own process a long time before and even had her credit card ready when it looked as if Stuart's had been refused. Later she had replacement forms for those he'd filled in too honestly—and then she packed everything up and air-freighted all of Batch 13's documents to China immediately, at her own cost. Roberta, Stuart later relayed, was genial and full of smiles; a wonderful blonde earth mother who probably should have had a dozen kids.

So finally the paperwork was finished, fares were booked and a date was set—but I still hadn't met anyone in the group.

'I think it's a good idea,' suggested Stuart. Batch 13 wanted to find out what to expect in China from a couple who'd completed the process. 'You go, Baby Boy,' I muttered from my computer. My nerves were jangling and it wasn't just because of the 'damned script' as it was now christened. I felt incredibly anxious and deeply apprehensive. What if our new child didn't like me? What if she came between Stuart and me, as the DoCS seminars had shown could happen? My mind is active at the best of times but it was now in chaos: why too wasn't I excited? Why didn't I look at the photo and melt? What if . . . what if . . .

'Only worry when you have reason to,' said Stuart as off he went—again, on his own. It was the first time he'd meet them all.

A few hours later when he walked back in the door I wanted every detail and grilled him with question after question like a relentless tormentor from the Spanish Inquisition. 'Oh they were okay,' he said, making himself a cup of tea, about to go up to his office as if he really thought this could suffice.

Stuart's introverted nature can only take so much socialising. He needed a break—but he wasn't going to get it on this occasion. 'But what were they like?' I pleaded, desperate to know who I would be travelling with.

'Like people who are excited about having a child. They're all childless.'

'But what do they do, what do they look like, how old are they, were they interesting?'

'I thought you didn't give two hoots about them,' he chipped back with a grin.

'Women are from Venus and men really are from Mars,' I thought to myself as he started talking. My account would have been one of hypothesis, impression, dissection and speculation. Stuart's droned on like a shopping list.

The baby had been asleep when they arrived. They had to be quiet. It was hot. The hostess was hospitable. The women wanted to see her sleeping baby. When she awoke they went to pieces. The wives exchanged photos of their soon-to-be daughters. One took out a 17-page checklist filled with questions like: 'Do you think it's a good idea to take cotton buds?' Predominantly the men kept quiet.

Finally Stuart said, exhausted, 'They're intrigued by you though.'

'Why?' I asked, surprised.

'Well it's the weekend, all six of them were there, but still it's only me turning up. They all expected to meet you. I can see some of them wondering if you actually exist.' We laughed heartily before he scurried off to his silence, leaving me to ponder. The date was imminent; Batch 13 would get to meet me soon enough.

At our celebratory leaving party one of my girlfriends said, 'You'll be a mummy!'

'Oh my God,' I thought to myself, 'it *really is* going to happen!'

CHAPTER 6

NOTHING IS WHAT IT SEEMS

Stuart

For Sharon there had been real doubts, but these were fuelled by fear of the unknown. I knew because she'd been seeking reassurance almost daily and showing major signs of cracking. Sharon is the most passionate of beings. Her capacity for joy is boundless and her energy, spark and wit are vibrant tonics for others, even when she's under the hammer. She's a motivator without peer and her antennae are always out and rarely fail her. She's the one to follow. But on the day of departure she was not at her best. 'We're going to China,' she said. 'What the hell for?'

On the plane Sharon's nerves were at cracking point. I felt a flood of relief when finally the drinks were served. 'Gin 'n Tonic!' she demanded. The air hostess was actually looking at me, but Sharon needed a drink and was not to be ignored.

'I'll have two,' I said, smiling nicely at the air hostess, secretly thinking, 'because I know I won't see you again for hours.' While congratulating myself on my foresight a sharp blow landed in my ribs.

'Why didn't you say you were going to ask for two? I would have asked for two.' Sharon hates to be shortchanged and this was a serious situation. 'Get her back, go on, go on!' Before I could say anything Sharon, who's not quite five foot, was up, craning over her seat with the menace of a ravenous buzzard that's spied a rotting carcass: 'Excuse me,' she hollered over the heads of passengers to the hostess who was now way down the aisle. 'Hello! I'll have another one as well thank you.'

After we polished off the drinks we began to relax. It had taken over three years to get to this point. Over three absurd years of bureaucratic nonsense.

Our nerves were on edge as we'd both given up smoking in a blood pact 14 hours earlier, but after another round of drinks our apprehension was displaced by a thrilling new-found confidence. We were on a great adventure and aglow at the prospect. So we didn't know anything about the child—what prospective parent ever does? Of course there were potential problems with her being almost two, speaking another language, adoption trauma, ethnic difference, grief, middle-aged parents and unknown hereditary traits, but so what! This was a new beginning, it was good and all was right with the world; she was an orphan who needed a home, and we were a 'home' that needed a child.

To my surprise our hostess expertly serviced our drinking rhythm unasked and with a wink and a nod. Full of bluster we strode on as one, sure we had all the answers on raising children. 'People make it hard for themselves.' 'We won't.' 'No, we won't,' we proclaimed, overlapping each other a little too loudly for the comfort of slumbering passengers nearby.

'Spoil them and you make a rod for your own back,' said Sharon, desperately burrowing in her bag for a Nicabate.

'No I know—love and boundaries,' I muttered through my teeth, sucking hard on an Anticol.

'Nothing could be more certain,' agreed Sharon, who'd come up empty on the Nicabate search.

Suddenly we stopped talking. Lately I'm leading and Sharon is following and this feels so strange. It's a REALLY BIG THING she's doing. Let's face it, she's freaking out. It's a big thing for me too, but nothing like it is for her. Usually I just roll with the waves that come along while Sharon actively shapes and spaces them, but it's not like that now. She's got this question bouncing around like a pinball in her brain: 'Do I really know what I'm doing?'

Alec and Pru (pseudonyms), another quarter of Batch 13, were on our flight from Hong Kong to Nanning, China. Alec, mid 40s, was a tall, fit livewire. He was a professional communicator and it showed as he spruiked enthusiastically, all the while listening closely to every word you said, grinning and leaning towards you. Like so many Englishmen his quick mind was always in search of a laugh and speedy, interactive discourse. He was perfect for Sharon and they laughed together heartily, but it all flew by too fast for my ponderous mind. So the two extroverts, Sharon and Alec, sparred ever so genially, while sizing each other up ever so carefully on the shuttle to the plane.

Pru was pretty sharp too, but more in my tempo. Also in her 40s, she was blonde and beautifully groomed, her perfectly fitting clothes accentuating an attractive mannequin's body. Her arm was in a sling because of mysterious shooting pains that had come out of nowhere. 'Anxiety may be to blame,' she volunteered, conscious of the irony that she was a professional hypnotherapist. Pru was interested, interesting and very forthright. Although less demonstrative than Alec she was firmly in charge.

These two were bubbly, warm and cheeky and Sharon immediately revised the level of involvement we might have with the others. 'Roberta Clapton has put her back out,' they told us, and Sharon began to sense she was not alone with her fears and worries.

Nanning was comfortably spread out after Hong Kong. It's an industrial provincial capital and a regional trade centre of a little over 1 million, with pretty touches here and there. Famously it was a major staging post for the North Vietnamese during the Vietnam War. Now it's mostly functional buildings and big wide streets with pushbikes, motorbikes, cars and small trucks incredibly interweaving without incident. Strangely, there was not a dog or cat anywhere in sight. Sometime later we discovered that in many parts of China, walking a pet dog is a status symbol paraded by the well-heeled. We also discovered that the culinary specialty of Nanning, in China's Guangxi Province, is Dog Hotpot, or 'Woof Woof' as it's also known.

'Oh my God, look!' I heard Sharon and Pru squeal in unison. As I fumbled with our passports at the five-star Majestic Hotel check-in, I saw the first one with his stroller out of the corner of my eye—a middle-aged, 18-stoner from the States with an ever-so-tiny Chinese baby girl. Then there were three. When I looked up again it had become a massive swirl of Busby Berkley choreography using the grand hotel foyer as a stage, but moments later we were alone again. It was an astonishing ballet of new dads with their tiny girls which flashed by so quickly I wondered whether it had happened at all. But it came back again and again and again.

It was bizarre watching the previous weeks' intake from all around the world with their new Chinese daughters, all in strollers, figure-eighting and circling in and out of the grand foyer—hundreds of them in the one hotel, and this in a small city by Chinese standards. But just below the surface of this surreal sight was a human reality of love, fun, screaming and tears.

Yes, it's almost always a girl. The one-child policy plays a big part in this, as does the firm tradition that children must look after their parents in old age—something daughters can't do, as they become members of the family into which they marry. To top it all, a deep reverence for one's ancestors insists a boy is there to preserve entrenched, patrilineal tradition.

These days the imbalance of the sexes is at crisis point in many parts of China with millions of young men adrift, unable to marry as there simply aren't enough women to go around. The shortage is so acute that kidnapping is common in many provincial areas.

Sharon was improving remarkably in the 'adoption environment' and the new-found company of Batch 13. We drank in the Spanish Quarter, which I so-dubbed because only the Spanish stay up with their kids and they do it in the bar. Good on them. But away from the bar I wasn't travelling as well. At this point I was really on edge: what was I thinking trying to give up smoking with emotional all-sorts all around? The hotel foyer suddenly exploded again, like a disturbed ants' nest this time; a weird conglomerate of huge dads and tiny babies diffusing in all directions before clumping again. 'Charging aimlessly,' I thought to myself. 'God, take a deep breath, that'll be you in a couple of days.'

Our hotel room was 'old world' and spacious, but all I saw was the tiny, empty, metal baby cot. Painted a baby blue with a pink blanket and a sheet over a piece of cardboard for a mattress, it was strategically placed alongside our bed. The adrenaline pump in my body went up ten notches. Soon it would no longer be just the two of us.

Sharon always insists you look directly at her if she's talking, not over your shoulder to see who else is around, not out the window, nor off in the distance. No-one is exempt. World leaders, movie stars and the Dalai Lama will all be brought swiftly into line or asked to move on if they fail in this. But as I spoke, struggling with the bags in the doorway, Sharon's head rigidly froze looking steadfastly at me, while her eyes flashed in morse-code rhythm towards the cot—white–dark–white– white–dark–white–dark . . . In the end I sat on the bed next to the cot to make things more comfortable for both of us.

'Let's go for a walk,' Sharon suggested, needing to calm frayed nerves. By the roadside I was distracted by a cyclist who was so laden it beggared belief. Dwarfed by massive sacks on all sides he strained ever so slowly for a single rotation, painful progress measured in inches up a modest incline as the swift current of traffic surged around every which way, ten wide along a six-lane boulevard.

'What are you doing?' screamed Sharon as I gazed at the cyclist. A charging truck belching thick black exhaust missed us by centimetres, the cadence of its blaring horn arcing with Doppler effect as its thin meniscus of pressured air bounced us firmly back to the kerb. Red or green, there seemed no way across this flood.

'No, no, you're mad!' Sharon wailed again as I grabbed her and jumped in once more. Reliving past football glory I sprinted, stopped and sprinted again, jigging and jagging into gaps like a warrior in a computer game. I retreated as motorbikes whizzed within inches then scampered ahead, forcing hooting cars and groaning trucks to alter course.

'Jesus Christ!' Sharon exclaimed on the far side. 'How the hell are we going to get back?'

Downstairs at the Majestic, East met West at breakfast with a sumptuous feast ranging from steaming congee to sizzling bacon. Here, amid a cacophony of wailing Chinese babies and fraught Western parents, our better-than-our-wildest-dreams guide, Kylie (pseudonym), introduced herself to us, and to Pru and Alec. Kylie was a good listener, a good talker and she understood everything. She was calm but enthusiastic and after seven years in the Middle East her English was excellent. Originally from a farming family, she escaped the vicious cycle of poverty through education and was now well married, with a boy. In a flash she arranged to take us to the 'finding sites' of our adoptive children, even though she wasn't supposed to. 'Take pictures,' she told us. 'When you come back to show your baby, everything will be gone. You will not recognise it even if you come back in a year.'

Pru and Alec's baby had been left just down the road at a children's hospital. As soon as we jumped out of the taxi Pru accosted a local woman with a baby on her back, asking all sorts of questions while Alec documented all on video. The woman didn't have a clue what was going on, but Pru carried on regardless: 'Me baby too,' she boomed in a well-spoken English accent, as if volume and over-enunciation would make a difference. Pru continued with some rapid-fire questions and then, happy she'd made 'contact' with another mother, moved on, leaving the poor dumbfounded woman rooted to the spot. We left Alec and Pru behind and moved on. After two hours of bumpy travel we reached the river. Shrouded in midday mists, this was the backward and impoverished rural China we weren't meant to see. The people were unspeakably poor, with filthy bare feet and hands, brown, broken teeth and torn, wintry clothing. The men ogled Sharon as if they'd never seen a white woman before.

These were Jia-Mei's people, but Sharon was fearful and intimidated by their scrutiny. At the river crossing she reluctantly got out of the cab, but in the open it was worse. Everyone just gaped at her, all gums and stumpy teeth, and a sense of menace was in the air. 'This is bloody pointless,' urged Sharon out of Kylie's earshot. 'This'll do, right here. Jia-Mei won't know where she came from anyway and her mother could be from anywhere. Let's just take some photos now and be done with it.' I agreed heartily, but God only knows what was going through our heads at the time; we wouldn't dream of such a casual approach to the child's heritage now. But I remembered that Kylie was taking a big risk for us and we couldn't let her down. In the end her excited face won the day and we punted across the river and ploughed on.

Suddenly we were on a massive 12-lane super highway in the making, carved out of the forest and edged by huge hills of stone, rubble and gravel. Here was a small sniff of China's breakneck development, but in this backwater we were the only vehicle in sight. Abruptly, after just a few hundred metres, this 'highway to nowhere' narrowed to a dirt track once more as it threaded into a village.

'This is it,' said Kylie as we pulled up outside a slightly grubby three-storey government building. Three girls and a boy used the forecourt as a playground. They were rugged up in thick orange parkas despite the mild spring weather, and greedily posed for Sharon's camera and our offer of a few sweets. The eldest girl was especially pretty. What would Jia-Mei be like?

Looking back we're so glad we persevered. We stood on the actual spot where Jia-Mei was found, the spot where her mother had been, the spot where all our lives intersected. And while this 'finding site' is probably of no account to anyone but us, the brutal, cement steps of the building where a desperate mother left her newborn to the mercy of others is the unprepossessing scene of great human tragedy.

Perhaps she abandoned Jia-Mei at cock-crow, still wet from the birth with umbilical cord attached, to ensure the medical staff found her quickly. Perhaps she had lingered for a long time, gazing at her child asleep in her arms, tears streaming down her face, choking back sobs in the darkness and, when she heard someone coming, fled into the fields. What was in this mother's heart? Surely her last act was an act of love when with trembling hands she pinned Jia-Mei's name to her chest—Beautiful Plum Blossom.

In the village where Jia-Mei was found bicycles were aplenty and a solitary truck, dating back 40 years, was proudly parked at one end. Somehow the earthen-floored buildings were at odds with the lay of the land, and all on the low side of the steeply cambered road were surely regularly flooded.

At the edge of the village the 12-lane super highway in the making threatened like a predator. Perhaps construction is now complete and this trace of Jia-Mei's beginnings has gone forever.

The rest of Batch 13 arrived from their flights that afternoon and we arranged to meet in the bar for a sundowner or two. On our left were the robust Super Correspondent Roberta Clapton and her youthful husband, Norman (pseudonym), opposite the lively and flirtatious Alec and Pru, and on our right the diminutive Beth (pseudonym), the self-described 'reluctant Yank' originally from New Jersey, and her tall, lean husband, croaky Christopher (pseudonym). Pinned against the back wall, Sharon and I primed ourselves for the fray. After a few drinks the group was merry; none more than Sharon, who was by now a bosom buddy with all the girls.

We finally dined and most of us were drinking more than we normally would, strangers together in a common enterprise, nervous as hell. Sharon and Alec were particularly lively and I probably wasn't far behind. I do remember that all the other women were vegetarians, vegans even, in contrast to the omnivorous Sharon who likes a large T-bone just waved over a flame, served in a pool of blood.

It was an incredible night, a night of honesty, hilarity and burgeoning friendship as four childless couples shared the unique experience of knowing that in two days they would be parents.

The next day Pru's arm wasn't getting any better, and Roberta's back was stuffed. Beth looked nervy and anxious, but Sharon was suddenly in the zone: 'Bring it on!'

CHAPTER 7

FIRST CONTACT
Sharon

'Bloody hell, Stuart, this is surreal!' I muttered, heart pounding, stomach churning. 'There's actually going to be a baby in there.' We both eyed the empty cot, gulping whooshes of air.

We had been awake since 5 a.m.; incomprehension, exhilaration and apprehension lay thick in the air. Finally, after years of waiting, this was it—the day that life as we knew it would change forever. Soon someone else's child would be placed in our arms—a child with a history. Taking another deep breath Stuart passed me a mint. His hands fumbled with the wrapper. His jacket was askew and a red rash was rising like molten lava over his face.

In the foyer downstairs Batch 13 was just as jumpy. 'Oh my God!', 'Shit!', 'Unbelievable!' Stuart was too nervous to speak and kept pretending to check the paperwork while I babbled with knife-edged excitement to anyone within earshot.

'I won't be able to carry her,' Pru lamented when I came up for air, her buggered arm now out of its sling. 'Alec!' she called stridently. 'I can't carry her!' But Alec, clutching his video camera like a comfort toy, was rapidly firing jokes to no-one in particular in a strangled, squeaking voice. Beth and Christopher stood stiffly mute with fixed smiles on their faces while Roberta again and again checked the contents of her baby bag as husband Norman stood to the side bewildered; a shag on a rock.

Abruptly Kylie arrived in an authoritative flurry and we were on the bus ripping through the streets of Nanning. My mind was reeling as we whizzed past cyclists, pedestrians and shabby, rundown Chinese dress shops. I couldn't do anything but clutch Stuart's hand. Now our highly talkative group was silent. It was a silence I have never known. We knew this experience would bond us together forever; beyond imagining it was exhilarating and terrifying. Within an hour we'd be back on this bus with four little girls—four total strangers—sitting on our laps.

The children were all from the same orphanage and only half a year apart. The two youngest were 14 months old; the next one up was 18 months and Jia-Mei, at 20 months, was the oldest. Only Jia-Mei had been named by her mother, the others had been named by the orphanage. Naming a child is important in China, but abandonment is a crime, so parents are reluctant to leave a note in fear of being traced. Yet Jia-Mei's mother had run this risk, pinning a name on her daughter's baby clothes to leave the only connection that she could.

'Can you believe it, the children are actually here, in the building,' said Pru. It was all too much for me and I cuddled tightly into Stuart, who kissed the top of my head and squeezed my hand.

'Congratulations, your children will be here soon,' was the

curt translation of an official's meandering speech in Mandarin that stretched for ten interminable minutes. Then, just like that, we heard the patter of tiny feet.

'I saw Jia-Mei!' yelled Pru pointing to one of the open doors. 'She was walking!' Then complete silence. No-one dared to breathe. Then a terrible, solitary wail, fit to wake the dead, as four little girls were carried in by their Chinese carers.

'That'll be mine,' I shouted to the others, pointing out the distraught wailer whose earth-shattering screams were piercing the room. Sure enough Jia-Mei was brought over, screeching, squirming, arching her back, writhing and kicking so hard it was a battle to hold her. The other children were a little shell-shocked but totally calm. Stuart fumbled in the baby bag, bringing out the tiny woodland creature we had bought in Hong Kong. Dressed in a blue satin Chinese outfit, the little woodland creature had reminded me of Jia-Mei with its thick mat of bushy, tufted hair. She seized it in between wails, clutching it tightly to her chest and never let it go throughout our stay in China.

'Poor little mite,' I said as flailing arms connected with my face. Tears poured onto quivering red lips and mixed with gurgling saliva: 'She's boiling over!' Even though it was warm, Jia-Mei was dressed in layer upon layer as she might be for a snowfield frolic. Perhaps this was simpler than packing a bag. Her clothes were stained and rumpled and as I looked at the grubby, garish, salmon-pink two-piece nylon suit with fake leopard fur around the sleeves, hood and cuffs, it tugged my heart to think this was probably her best. Under this a pale blue and black jumper covered a sleeveless black and orange woollen vest, which in turn covered a thick sweatshirt above a singlet. Her tiny red cloth shoes were grimy, the only ones she ever owned judging by the stench of urine. Her hair, unwashed, was greasy and matted. On her face nasty scabs from a recent fall made me hold her close in maternal protection.

But Jia-Mei was having none of it. She fought hard, shrieking like a wild animal caught in the sharp teeth of a bear trap. Glimpsing the others smiling and cooing over quiet, dazed babies my maternal confidence was in tatters. 'Your turn buster,' I said to Stuart, bundling the screaming banshee over to him. She immediately calmed down and my humiliation was complete. I wanted to hit Stuart over the head with a rock and then crawl under it as a gamut of emotions swelled through my body. In panic I once again recalled the DoCS seminars and the story of the child who'd wedged herself between the parents by rejecting her adoptive mother.

'So that's why I had a bad feeling,' I thought to myself irrationally.

But Jia-Mei had just been getting her breath. Recharged, she sobbed and screamed all over town as yet more bits of paper changed hands. She wailed and wailed on the bus and at the official photo shoot, all the while clutching the woodland creature. Back at the hotel, the wailing continued. Stuart too looked stunned. 'Poor bugger,' I thought as I surveyed his desperate eyes and scaly face. He was falling apart. Giving up smoking had been a lot easier for me but that, combined with this emotional nightmare, was taking a heavy toll. No matter what we tried the screaming persisted, so I took out a sleeping tablet—and, knocking it back with three beers, left Stuart to it.

'Stuart, remember the photos we sent to China?' I asked, shaking the little woodland creature at Jia-Mei, whose up-tempo screams had reached new heights. The room looked like a battlefield with baby bottles, nappies and clothes strewn everywhere. 'Green's a very unlucky colour in China, read what it says,' I told him, thrusting a magazine article in his face. 'I was wearing green in the photos!'

'Oh for Christ's sake, Sharon, that's it!' yelled Stuart. It did seem a ridiculous notion, but why hadn't I taken to the photo like all the others? Why did this baby cry when none of the others did? I just didn't know what to do and felt convinced my life was over. By now the din was deafening. No matter what I did, she just wouldn't stop crying. After hours of it I began to wail too. I cried for all the longing and pain I'd gone through to have a child; tears of inadequacy and fear. I wailed and wailed. By this time Stuart had developed a psoriatic rash across both hands.

I was into my second hour of wailing and contemplating going back to Sydney to rent a one-bedroom flat when I realised something was different. Jia-Mei was standing bolt upright, leaning over her cot, staring at me with seriously perplexed eyes. I stared back at her, my swollen eyes matching her own, and suddenly laughed, wiping the stream from my nose. 'Bah!' she said, hitting the air in front of me as if to say: 'Get a grip'. Now I was laughing like a crazed hyena, which made her stare even more. 'Ah,' I said to Stuart, 'look at her. She's so sweet.'

The next morning the emotional debris of the previous night's storm had ebbed and the seas were now tranquil. Jia-Mei, holding onto the bed, happily pounded a pillow while chewing on a rusk. Tears still welled in her eyes and occasionally she gasped in panic, but now her fear was mostly replaced by curiosity as she grabbed at things around her.

Coming out of the shower, Stuart announced he was going out to buy some toys. As the door closed behind him I looked in wonder at my new daughter, who stood gaping at the mirror intrigued by her reflection. This vulnerable, tiny child had come into our lives. She belonged to us now and we belonged to her. Captivated, she continually patted the mirror with her sticky hands, pushing her face close to see how the warm breath left a mist. I too was captivated and when her reflection disappeared behind smudges of spittle and condensation, and she bashed the mirror as if trying to get it to work again, a coruscating energy burst from my soul, leaving in its wake a warmth that washed over me from head to toe. What had I been thinking? My reaction to her photo had been nothing but fear. Stupid fears: what if she was hard to deal with; what if she had horrible character traits; what if, what if . . . When I had first seen the other children's photos I had wanted any one of them but Jia-Mei. Now watching her, I wanted no other but her. A tingle went up my spine as again I marvelled, not quite able to comprehend: she was mine—this small child, so dependent, standing in just a nappy, was mine. Finally, after her bashing had failed, she shrivelled her eyes and gave me an evil-eyed glare. I didn't know it then but in those moments the first seeds of love between us were sown.

I wiped the mirror for her, she became captivated once more, and when it misted over, I wiped it again. At some point in this game my own reflection surfaced. I might have been swooning on the inside but on the outside I looked like I'd done 12 rounds with a heavyweight: eyes still swollen and red, face blotched. I was yet to shower and my hair, matted from tears, was stuck like a cap to my throbbing head.

'Hello!' It was Pru, perky as hell and knocking on my door. Feeling wretched I ignored it. The knocking became a persistent bashing. 'I know you're in there, I can hear youuuu!' she shouted. 'Open up, come on, open up!' Somewhat vexed, I flung the door wide. Pru waltzed in with her new daughter.

Immediately my eyes took in Alec, who was sitting on the bed in the room directly opposite. Pale and unkempt, his body hung limp, half bent, dispirited. 'She was up all night,' Pru announced with a tremulous edge. 'She won't let me out of her sight. She wants me to carry her. I can't carry her. She keeps screaming if I don't but I can't, how can I?' She rattled like an automaton for several minutes and, as abruptly as she had entered, left. I watched her waltzing down the corridor, mumbling like a deranged sleepwalker and knocking on another door.

Knowing I was not the only traumatised soul, my spirits lifted—and so did Jia-Mei's when Stuart returned with a hastily purchased, battery-operated 'Big Chick' that sang nifty jingles in Mandarin. For the first time smiles and pure fun descended between us all.

But Jia-Mei didn't really smile. Kylie said she was just a serious child. Quiet, she would peer at you from her tight, little face that was yet to relax into the beauty she would become. If we attempted to cuddle her, a securely clenched baby-fat fist would be placed firmly between her body and ours. When she was carried her arms and legs would dangle like a rag doll's. But with the Big Chick and the misty mirror game there'd been progress, and after the second day I was dancing with her and blowing up balloons. In between times Stuart started holding her for long periods on the enclosed window ledge so she could see the bustle of the street below, all the while singing to her quietly. Eventually, the heaving chest and the terror of it all had just about subsided and, to our great relief, a blissful, soothing, calm descended, as it does in the eye of a hurricane.

'Christ, she's been beaten!' I screamed to Stuart, looking at the mass of overlapping blue bruises covering Jia-Mei's tiny body as she sat solemn-faced in her bath. 'Oh my God, that's disgusting, no wonder she cried so much, poor little thing. How could anyone do this to a child? The bastards!'

'They don't seem to cause her any pain,' said Stuart as he gingerly touched them, and then announced it would do us all good to go out.

When we first entered the People's Park with Jia-Mei happy and snug in her stroller, an immediate sense of wellbeing swept over both of us. A large lake complete with island was crisscrossed by walkways and surrounded by beautiful trees, gardens and the springtime chatter of birds. It was warm but misty. Not far off, the tender, reflective song of a solitary *erhu* soothed our souls. And it was so still; a stillness unknown to coastal dwellers in our own wild continent. We took lots of photos so we could remember feeling spiritual.

'Is it a boy?' asked a strong male voice from behind us as we approached the middle of a small bridge laced by weeping willows. A well-dressed Chinese man was pointing at Jia-Mei. I was taken aback. It was a real surprise to hear someone speaking English. 'No, it's . . . she's a girl,' I said proudly.

'Why not get a boy?' he asked, stunned. When we explained China allocates the children, he pointed at Jia-Mei and started to snigger 'peasant baby'.

'You buy peasant baby, very gooood, very gooood,' he chuckled, ruffling Jia-Mei's hair. 'Buying Chinese baby, good thing, goood,' he said waving us off, laughing to himself. It was clear the last thing a local would do is adopt a girl from peasant stock.

Even Kylie, who had risen from village life, was shockingly disparaging. When we asked her whether farmers ever fostered children as so many abandoned girls came from the countryside, she dismissed this idea as silly. Farmers were too low in the scheme of things.

'Who does then?'

'Unemployed factory workers, that sort of thing,' she replied. As I surveyed my little girl's innocent face, her untamed hair and thick sturdy body, I was grateful for the chance to adopt her. People here despised her background and they also despised her gender.

Stuart's diary, 17 March 2004

Much to Sharon's relief Kylie explained about the Mongolian Spots—it's not bruising, just a pigmentation which will eventually fade. All the children have them.

We've turned the corner and I'm greatly encouraged. As each day passes more and more of Jia-Mei's personality emerges. What a revelation when we first sat down to eat. My God, can she ever wolf it down! A bowl of congee disappears in seconds to be followed by mountains of fruit and meat and cheese and rice. Anything she can lay her hands on.

Beth's right. The watermelon gave her diarrhoea but she's over that now. The formula thing scared me at first but I reckon I've got it down. She attacks her bottle as if her life depends on it.

The first day she just howled without stop. The second she was a stunned mullet but there was a dash of animation emerging. Now there's some humour with this evil-eye thing—she's thawing really fast considering how it all started between us.

Occasionally she's obstinate: that's got to be a good sign, a sign she's overcoming her fear. She's also got an independent streak—another good sign. The hardness has left her face a little, she's not exactly smiling but she will.

She is so beautiful in her new clothes, hair washed and cleaned up, wobbling unsteadily on chubby legs in a sort of dance to the perky Big Chick's chipmunk ditties. She lets me pick her up, but not for long.

A little patience, that's all that's needed. Sharon's over the initial shock and in full-flight mother mode. I think she's surprised herself—she's a natural. The two of them are steaming ahead now and all is well. I'm thrilled for us all.

As for me, I throw her in the stroller—she just loves being wheeled around—and join the throng of dads doing the same, weaving in and out of the grand foyer downstairs.

After our walk in the People's Park, I was curious to see how the others were faring and left the room door open pretending to Stuart I was letting air in. We'd been separated from the others for two full days and to my utter relief, we heard story after story of woe: doctors had been called, fathers had been rejected outright, one child hysterically thrashed in her stroller making going out impossible, another refused to ever get out of her stroller, making staying in somewhat silly. The normally ebullient Alec still looked totally spent and a very dejected Pru was constantly hounded by her terrified, bawling daughter to pick her up. So we were not alone; indeed we were faring better than most.

That night as Jia-Mei lay in her cot I sang the 'Skye Boat Song' and gently stroked her hair when she'd let me. It is a song my mother sang to me and it never failed to lull me into the deepest slumber. After two verses, the most almighty deep guttural gasp followed by a horrendous bellow and snort punctured the moment as Stuart, mouth agape, book smashed down on his face, fell into a rumbling, snoring semi-coma. 'Great,' I thought.

At midnight Jia-Mei was still perky and I wondered how much longer I could keep this singing up. By 1 a.m. I knew she'd got the better of me and I swept her into my arms ignoring her struggle, no longer caring how she felt, and placed her firmly between myself and the open-mouthed, rancid-breathed Stuart. 'She can take the brunt of his snores,' I thought—I couldn't care less and, turning into the pillow, promptly and without any remorse fell asleep.

CHAPTER 8

BEYOND THE ORPHANAGE

Sharon

It's taken for granted that it's a good thing to meet the foster mother/family of your child. So after our daughter had been ripped from her Chinese family and was just beginning to adjust to her new life, we were supposed to take her back to see her foster mother at the orphanage just one more time before we ripped her away again. I thought this was positively stupid. Surely it would have been better to do it all in one go at the very beginning.

Before we fully got off the bus, tall, croaky Christopher and his petite wife Beth were swamped. Their child was snatched away in a trice and instantly back in the arms of her Chinese foster family—dancing, singing, laughing and having a high time of it all. The others too were swamped. But there was no-one there to meet Stuart and me at all; no smiling face to greet Jia-Mei. We moved away and stood apart—an isolated, sad pair with its small child, looking on. I pulled Jia-Mei close to the warm comfort of my body, leaning my chin on her stubbornly erect head. Instead of melting to the warmth, she remained stiff and inert. It appeared from her blank face she had no recognition of the place whatsoever.

Eventually we were herded into a huge conference room where families could talk using Kylie to interpret. Everyone in our group seemed to be laughing as foster carers and orphanage staff fussed over their respective children, providing much sought after information. We sat apart in a far corner. Jia-Mei on my lap played poignantly with her woodland creature. 'So much for my worrying over this meeting, she isn't even here,' I said to Stuart. 'Go and ask Kylie what the hell is going on.' New ferocious, protective feelings were rising in me. My child would not be ignored. Where was her foster mother?

Kylie came running over with the news that Jia-Mei's foster mother was on her way in a taxi, she'd come yesterday and got the days mixed up. 'Walk with me to see the little ones,' she said. We followed meekly like Brown's cows through renovations of little bridges over half-constructed waterways and lily ponds towards a brand-new building. Along the way labourers of all ages and sexes swept, shovelled and gardened in jumpers and overcoats in the 26 degree heat.

'It's all bloody odd,' I grumbled to Stuart, past caring who heard me. 'If she was here yesterday why didn't they tell her when to come back today?' Stuart wasn't bothered with questions, it was enough for him she was coming.

The new orphanage building smelled and looked like a clinic with its off-white tiles and walls. The staff wore white hospital gowns, their black hair tightly swept back. The only decoration was a mass of large red lanterns hanging from the ceiling. Off this area were the babies' rooms, which were incredibly quiet. Stuart and I walked ahead of the others and peeked into a room.

'Bloody hell,' I whispered to Stuart, fumbling with my camera.

'No photos,' explained Kylie. But Stuart and I had already seen what could not be photographed before the door was snapped shut. The room was a riot of unattended babies crawling over each other like maggots over meat.

From another room a nurse emerged pushing a cot on wheels. Inside were six small girls. They made a gruesome sight. 'Special needs,' said Kylie as we stared at the gaping holes between their noses and lips: cleft palates yet to be fixed. 'They are about to be adopted by American couples,' she said proudly. 'Come this way.'

Without warning Jia-Mei's foster mother appeared. In her late 30s with a wide friendly mouth, hair swept back and casually dressed, she seemed nervous. Suddenly I felt nervous and I could see Stuart did too. Remarkably, Jia-Mei had no immediate recognition. When her foster mother bent down smiling and stroked her face speaking to her in Mandarin, Jia-Mei stared blankly. We sat for a while and heard through Kylie routine stuff about food and sleep and favourite things while the foster mother held Jia-Mei for the last time. She had brought gifts of miniature milks and picture books in Chinese. We heard that Jia-Mei loved picking out her foster mother's clothes and bringing the paper to her foster father.

'She is a very good baby,' we heard, 'very, very good.'

I wanted to know why Jia-Mei scrunched up her face, giving us 'the evil-eye'. The foster mother laughed and said she was mimicking her myopic foster father who taught her that as a joke. Then suddenly it was all too much and the foster mother started sobbing. To my surprise tears were also running down my tense cheeks and finally Jia-Mei, who often seemed a bit slow on the uptake, howled and howled. Kylie jumped up and strode away purposefully and without sentiment: 'The others are waiting,' she said over her shoulder on her way out.

I followed as Stuart carried Jia-Mei back in his arms. Across the new grounds under construction, along dusty, winding paths and over little bridges we walked, not daring to look back on the clearest and sunniest day of our visit. But I did look back for a few seconds just as we reached the labourers in their coats. Jia-Mei was still howling and her foster mother had ventured down the path just far enough to see Jia-Mei's departure for as long as possible. Tears were streaming down her face as she plaintively waved a white handkerchief and edged a step or two closer. I grabbed Jia-Mei from Stuart, took her tiny hand, and waved back to the woman who'd torn across town in a taxi for a final five minutes with the baby she'd nurtured for the last 18 months.

I tried to tell her with my eyes and arms that Jia-Mei will be safe with us. That she will be loved as she has been loved. That the connection with her will never be broken, that the red threads are alive and well between us all. I took a couple of steps towards her and looked peacefully into her distant eyes. No longer waving, she nodded in understanding, pressed her palms together in front of her, and lightly bowed to me. I passed the distraught Jia-Mei back to Stuart, smiled, pressed my hands together and bowed in return.

Stuart grabbed Jia-Mei's hand and started waving it again as he retreated towards the bus. Jia-Mei's foster mother waved back exuberantly. The path took a sharp bend now and we slid out of sight. A little further on, the trees thinned and I could just make out the foster mother, on my left in the distance, still waving her white handkerchief frantically and edging up the path as far as she dared.

The others were waiting in the bus and as we settled in, Jia-Mei howled like a demon, her heart breaking. 'At least we know she was loved,' Stuart said softly. But as the bus pulled away, I thought, 'There's more to it than that.' None of the other children were crying; they were playing happily on their mother's laps. Yet my baby's love for her former carer was not easily forgotten and even though her distress broke my heart and I did all that I could to soothe her, a warm glow filled my soul. Jia-Mei wasn't just loved, she loved back deeply in return. She was just like me.

It's curious how parents always search for their own character in their children. Interestingly, it is no different with an adopted child. I once asked Stuart if he could love an adopted child like he did his own daughter, Jo. He replied without hesitation: 'Yes.' I had doubted him. But now, pulling Jia-Mei's small, trembling body into the comforting warmth of mine, I understood. She *was* my child.

Stuart's diary, 19 March 2004
Today after lunch we were taken to a farming community and the unspeakable poverty there knocked me for six. We've all seen this stuff on TV but to see it in the flesh is another thing altogether. What hit me more than anything was the joylessness of it all. Every face was hard and sombre as if they were all on their way to the gallows. Life appeared to be without hope, without the prospect of advancement of any type, as it is for Sisyphus. And life was clearly very hard.

The buildings were virtually empty: no furniture, dirt floors, a few mats. Maybe they were more for the animals than the people. A dilapidated, antiquated tractor was parked by one of the houses. Old women sat outside their homes as others, carrying buckets on ropes and sticks bent to near breaking, continued blank-faced with their daily chores. I wondered whether one of these grim-faced women staring stonily ahead, taking baby steps as she carried her back-breaking burden, could have been Jia-Mei's mother. 'The orphans are the lucky ones,' one of Sharon's Chinese students told us. Maybe they are.

It was overcast again and that didn't help—mud was everywhere and everyone was covered in filth. Many layers of filth. I felt guilty parading my affluence in front of them. I felt guilty that our four Chinese orphans were dressed in pink and white frilly party dresses.

'Most of your children would have come from areas like this,' Kylie had said as we rolled off the tour bus in our neatly pressed Western clothes and designer shades clutching top-of-the-range digital cameras trying hard not to muddy our shoes.

I wondered how so many of us in Australia have so much but can only rue our lot, can only see problems and hardship ahead. No, I wasn't prepared for how it would affect me. I couldn't look anyone in the eye, I had to look away.

Ironically, after the first couple of days, Jia-Mei had turned into the most placid child imaginable. Wherever we took her she sat quietly occupying herself for hours leafing through a book or drawing on paper. If she had food to eat as well she was ecstatic. Like many orphanage children she ate whatever you put in front of her, like a Mexican bandit in a western. We both saw that as a good sign, that she was becoming more relaxed.

So followed halcyon days of brand-new children, brand-new clothes and shiny new mamas and dadas beaming with pride and love as their children, with tears still glistening in their eyes, smelled new food, did new exciting things and slowly, ever so slowly, thawed out.

For Stuart though there was just one worry. Jia-Mei could stand okay but she didn't seem capable of walking properly. She spent long periods frozen to the spot, especially in front of the low mirror near the front door, one foot firmly planted in front of the other. So up and down our hotel corridor he would walk her, taking Big Chick with him singing its jingles. And from almost every door of the sprawling wide corridors of the Majestic Hotel he heard babies crying. This was the 'adoption' floor. Daily, new groups arrived as others left, and behind closed doors hundreds of new parents were trying to soothe and take terror away. Walking might have been an issue for Jia-Mei, but we were very happy our new daughter was now out of step with the rest.

Every morning we joined hundreds of couples from Spain, Portugal, France, England, America and Australia who congregated to eat breakfast with their newly acquired Chinese girls. On our last morning in Nanning, Stuart went to get more food for our rapacious eater. Suddenly Jia-Mei's face dropped. What was wrong? I offered her some of my bacon and eggs. She knocked it away. Now I was sure something was terribly wrong. With quivering lips she raised her tiny body out of her highchair, craning her neck around the room, her eyes alive with panic. Her little arms shook as she raised herself higher and higher and on the verge of tears her face began to contort with fear. Still in the highchair she clambered to her feet and I rushed to support her. 'What's wrong, little one?' I whispered as she twisted from my grasp to turn towards the kitchen area, her trembling body vibrating in my arms.

When Stuart came into view laden with food and full of smiles she slumped back down, relieved, but never once took her eyes off him until he sat down. It was the first moment she had shown an attachment to either of us—indeed it was the first emotional response I'd seen other than brute distress—and as I ruffled her hair and kissed her baby cheeks I felt a delicious inner glow. I was now the person she went to most. If she felt that for Stuart, she felt it for me, and for the first time I felt the delectable warmth that only love can bring to a family.

Jia-Mei continued to be no trouble at all. At the end of the week she took the flight to Guangzhou in her stride like a veteran. After landing, the airport was a massive crush and she didn't bat an eyelid. Groups of 50 or 100, including huge groups of Westerners with babies, had arrived en masse to organise—like us—the consulate paperwork necessary to bring our babies home.

Our new guide, Han Pho, insisted on using the bus microphone even though we only occupied the first four rows. He was a perky character. 'Call me "hand phone",' he urged as he waved his mobile in the air. Despite his youth he reminded me of the unemployed vaudevillians in Woody Allen's *Broadway Danny Rose* as he cracked jokes that fell as flat as pancakes. Our polite laughter soon waned and we just stared mindlessly out the window, but Jia-Mei was mesmerised. She couldn't take her eyes off him. Her scrutiny was focused, serious and intense. It was as if only she really understood him.

As we checked in to our hotel a light misty rain began to fall. It was the sort of rain I'd always associated with China even though I'd never been there before—the rain of an ancient civilisation—and when we walked the modern, polluted streets of Guangzhou it seemed this rain was all that remained of China's distant past.

But mostly we stayed put in the hotel. We were all tired and strung out, marking time and desperate to get home and draw our children close. After four days the paperwork was finally done and we were back on the airport bus, where Han Pho took it upon himself to sing to us en route from his vast supply of strident karaoke hits. We applauded the first effort appreciatively, but by the fourth there was dead silence. By his eighth number cat calls of cruel derision greeted every line and he was pelted by missiles from all sides. He then paused, broke his artistic pose, soaked up what he saw as accolade, thanked us from the bottom of his heart and commenced his encore.

Once again Jia-Mei couldn't take her eyes off him and when he bent down to speak to her, her gaze penetrated his very core. It was eerie. You could see he was perplexed and a little unnerved but he shrugged the weirdness of it off and bounced back with a final flurry of self-promotion. He was desperate to impress and to impress upon us his overwhelming desire to become an Australian resident. At this point Jia-Mei abruptly lost interest and diverted her attention to her woodland creature. She knew the show was over. It was over for all of us too. We were weary and more than ever just wanted to go home.

We'd been uncharacteristically silent as we boarded the plane. 'We're taking them away,' lamented Pru. 'I feel horrible, this is their home.' We understood what she meant. Somewhere on this soil walked the biological parents of our babies, the link to their past. But according to Chinese lore, it was not about us. From the moment they were born their red threads had been cast way off shore into a raging river that would carry them thousands of miles to a completely different world, away from their heritage, away from their birthright because their destinies did not lie in their homeland.

Just after take-off the plane banked heavily and we all looked down at the relentless bustle of Guangzhou through the far windows. It was as if the pilot had decided to do a lap of honour for our little girls before leaving the mainland; his pronounced tilt held stubbornly. As the plane continued its arc and groaned for elevation I looked away from the big city and fixed on the sinking sun to the west through my own window, towards Nanning. Somewhere out there walked Jia-Mei's mother. How hard would it be to leave your baby in the night on a step and walk away? How torturous would it be to never know your child's fate? I tried to make contact with her in my mind; I tried to tell her Beautiful Plum Blossom was safe, that she would be loved.

After the plane levelled I saw a glimpse of the People's Republic retreating through gaps in the cloud and I hugged Jia-Mei close. The others did the same with their girls and, caught in the moment, we fixed on the diminishing shoreline, unblinking with moist eyes, and whispered a promise: 'We will return'.

INTERMEZZO

ANY PATIENT PAEDOPHILE WITHOUT A POLICE RECORD CAN ADOPT

Stuart

Before I had anything to do with the world of inter-country adoption I'd had a picture in my mind's eye of gentle people seeking children overseas, being kindly assisted by relevant authorities and together making something beautiful happen. For us and so many others, the reality proved very different. Today, even the very mention of DoCS (the NSW Department of Community Services) has couples raising their eyes as their lips tighten; others, their rage so great, are unable to speak. 'Don't get me started!' is the unanimous catch-cry.

In the past decade or so there was such a swell of discontent with DoCS' adoption procedures, typified by criticism from high-profile campaigner Deborra-Lee Furness, that in 2005 Senator Bronwyn Bishop led a parliamentary inquiry into the matter. Her report accused DoCS of actually having an 'anti-adoption' mentality. This is both bizarre and scary when they have a monopoly on the process. What was going on? While I can only speculate, the following account draws on our experience and that of many others.

DoCS was of course set up as a child protection agency. Then came the demand for international adoption, when local adoption basically dried up. With people marrying later infertility was on the rise, and the numbers looking to adopt swelled quickly. Suddenly DoCS found itself dealing with the general public in big numbers and it wasn't prepared.

In the midst of the clamour for overseas orphans, DoCS simultaneously had an acute shortage of foster parents for local children removed from their families, so in this context international adoption was not a priority. Its International Adoption Division languished with just a handful of junior staff and a lengthening queue at its door. Like an Indian bureaucracy there was paper everywhere, the same bits often lodged many times over in adjacent filing cabinets. In-trays were overflowing and well-meaning staff were caught between a rock and a hard place, with disaffected 'clients' on the one hand, and hopeless disorganisation, outmoded policy and antiquated systems on the other.

In this circumstance the scrutiny of the applicants was outsourced to freelance social workers. The upshot of this was another ocean of paper, as assessments were made only on the basis of reports. However, responsibilty for the adoptive children was still taken very seriously and, with only bits of paper to go on—albeit lots of them—great care was required before giving the final stamp of approval.

Most applicants had a galling wait of two or three years before they were processed.

It is likely that DoCS was aware that its process, which relied almost entirely on a solitary social worker's report, was less than perfect, so it decided to scare the daylights out of prospective parents in the seminars. If you got through these then at least it showed a level of commitment. Sadly, this lack of balance saw many decent people drop out before the process even started. What of the orphans who were missing out? It seems they just weren't part of the thinking.

Perhaps the long delay also served a purpose. No-one was in a hurry to fix it because it too meant that only the really committed would stick it out. 'Any patient paedophile without a police record can adopt from overseas,' we used to say—for patience, it seemed, was the only quality necessary.

When we returned from China with Jia-Mei back in March 2004 we immediately approached DoCS' International Adoption Division to adopt a second child. 'It can't be done,' they said simply. 'You have to wait 12 months before you can even fill in a form.'

One case manager who was pregnant at the time told Sharon empathetically over the phone: 'There's plenty of time. You can apply until you're 55. You just have to wait a year. Why don't you just concentrate on the one you've got?'

'That's what I am doing,' Sharon replied. 'She needs a sibling. I'm also concentrating on the child we may get in the future because she doesn't need grandparents; she needs a mother and a father.'

As in the TV series *Little Britain*, this was a world of 'computer says no'. There was no flexibility, just a stack of policies designed to defend against worst-case scenarios, rather than most-case scenarios. It took three and a half years to get Jia-Mei; God only knew how long it would take the next time round—and they wanted to add another year on top! Besides, does anyone ask a natural parent to wait a year before trying to conceive again? On top of this was the sure knowledge that tens of thousands of children were languishing throughout China, their small windows of opportunity closing fast while bureaucrats around the world fiddled.

We requested a meeting with DoCS to talk it out and to our surprise were granted one instantly. When we arrived, right on time, for the first time we went straight in without delay. A senior, older manager and our regular manager were there to greet us, tea and biscuits at the ready. Both had a weary air of condescension as they explained the facts of life to us. Their attitude was defensive, as if they'd weathered many storms before, and with that came an intractable 'brick wall' mentality.

On many queries they said their hands were tied, they had their instructions from parliament or departmental policy; 'It's been gazetted' they said over and over. This applied in particular to the one-year 'cooling off' period.

'So you don't agree with these provisions?' I asked.

'That's not what I said,' the senior manager replied, a little irritated. Perhaps they saw us as querulous people; perhaps they had mountains of work to get through; perhaps there really was nothing they could do, but they didn't seem to have any initiative or inclination for change, or any empathy for our position.

'Okay,' said Sharon. 'You know one of the things I don't quite understand is why you never contacted our referees. Surely an existing child would be of interest too, but Stuart's daughter, Jo, was never contacted. Sorry, but it doesn't make sense to me.'

'We read the referees carefully,' the young one said.

'But I could have written them *myself*,' Sharon replied with a wry smile.

81

'No, we make sure the handwriting's different.'

'I could have *dictated* them,' Sharon continued.

'Well we know they're your friends so they're unlikely to say anything critical,' the young one said, leaning forward for emphasis, smiling.

'So, for you, referees are a waste of time,' I chipped in.

'That's not what she said,' said the older one, annoyed.

Sharon moved on. She suggested that DoCS may not be aware of it but they fostered a culture of fear because of the ultimate power they wielded. Sharon thought they would like to know this and want to change it because when there's a culture of fear, people will never be able to open up properly and be honest. This in turn must make it much more difficult to assess applicants. If they're on their guard how can you ever know who they really are? Sharon thought they might like this feedback also to find ways to make the whole process less intimidating.

'There's not much we can do about that,' the older one said matter-of-factly.

Sharon tried another tack, concentrating this time on the second child. 'You know, I don't really understand the whole interview process at all. From what I've heard, if you don't have a medical issue or a police record then no-one is knocked back; is that right?'

'That's about right,' the older one said.

'You mean no-one's ever been knocked back?' asked Sharon in surprise.

'Well there *has* been one.'

'What happened?'

'They'd already adopted a child and were applying for another. They weren't fit to have a child.'

'What happened to the first child?'

'There was nothing we could do about that. They shouldn't have been allowed to adopt in the first place.'

'But what about the first child, was it left in their care?' Sharon persisted.

'Yes.'

'But that's terrible,' said Sharon, shocked. 'How could you leave it there?'

No-one replied and the manager glimpsed at her watch.

So, around and around in circles we went. Important questions were issues of policy 'over which we have no control', but they clearly agreed with the official line. They knew what was in the best interests of the child, they monotoned in a way that brooked no challenge. Clearly they'd never laid eyes on a Chinese orphanage, as we had.

When we left we felt we'd wasted our time. We knew they thought we'd wasted theirs. But to their credit, not long after, DoCS introduced some initiatives that made the process a little faster, especially for second-timers. Around the same time, their fees went up from around $1800 to approximately $10,000 for a first child, and $7000 for a second.

Part Two

CHAPTER 9

YOU CAN'T BUY THIS

Stuart

The next three months were three of the best I've ever had. Sharon was still working one day a week and battling an impossibly tight script deadline on a screenplay about a senior copper who'd been wrongly charged with multiple counts of rape. The ABC had taken out an option on it, and so had Screentime, the future producers of the *Underbelly* series. As a result, a fair bit of Jia-Mei's care in the early days fell to me. We lived slowly and the days drifted by pleasantly. I'd read the books: I didn't push Jia-Mei and didn't rush anything and ever so slowly she moved closer to me.

Jia-Mei still didn't like to be hugged and she didn't talk but we played cricket and soccer, watered the garden and wandered everywhere together. Because of Jia-Mei's fascination for water I got her a miniature watering can and over and over she splashed the paving stones, fascinated, seeing no point whatsoever in watering the plants—after all, that way you couldn't see what happened to the water. In no time we had the cleanest path in town.

I took her swimming in the protected baths below the Surf Life Saving clubhouse at Coogee and, keeping her safe in my arms, dunked her occasionally below the surface. She soon got over the shock and looked for more, but not too much more. I did the stuff blokes do with kids when their mothers aren't around. I let Jia-Mei try to climb trees and boulders. I let her explore and I encouraged her to run.

Whenever she could Sharon took a break from her writing and we showed Jia-Mei the sights of Sydney together. On these outings Jia-Mei only had to point at something and Sharon would be at the cash register in a flash. 'We won't spoil her,' we'd confidently trumpeted on the plane. Sure.

I'd had a child before and thought I was an old hand. But when I look back at the photos, seeing myself with Jia-Mei in those early days, it was just the same as it had been some twenty years earlier with Jo. My age and 'experience' didn't come into it. I was a 'young' thrilled father once again—smirking like an idiot, swamped by that mysterious gushing that inhabits first-time parents.

Jia-Mei had a large head plonked on a solid, squat, but tiny body and we laughed that Sharon's akubra was a perfect fit for her. A close cousin to a baby hobbit, she had thick, black, bushy hair and bright, shiny oval eyes, but her demeanour was deadly serious and her focus intense. She amazed me, being able to occupy herself for hours like no other child I'd ever seen. Above all she liked to draw, and as she drew squiggle after squiggle she rocked on her chair rhythmically oblivious to all around her. She loved picture books and leafed through them interminably, turning the pages quickly with her chubby little fingers like a patient in a doctor's waiting room with an old magazine. Bizarrely for a child under two, she made no demands at all. Had she spent most of her life alone, kept in a cot during the day until her foster parents returned after dark from work? I feared so.

With Magnus she was calm and kind and totally at ease, keen to feed him and stroke him ever so lightly.

A favourite spot was our local dog park, which follows the cliff edge just beyond the southern end of Coogee Beach. One afternoon I was there with Jia-Mei and Magnus as a stiff nor'-easter attacked with gusto and whitecaps stretched to the horizon. As usual, Magnus took no interest in the ball. 'What's in it for me?' he seemed to be thinking as he turned his head disdainfully before trotting off to the bushes, where he began to methodically mark out the entire 400-metre perimeter.

Jia-Mei on the other hand charged after the ball in a lumbering toddler's gait, tripping over every few steps. She was a terrible mover, and very slow, even for a toddler. Each time she bent down to pick up the ball, another gust rolled it a metre further on. Eventually she had it and turned back to me, poker-faced. I smiled warmly and applauded her success.

In the background some people smiled at Jia-Mei as they jogged by, muscles rippling, water bottle in hand. 'What a different world to Redfern,' I thought, 'where people went shopping in their dressing-gowns'. Here our two-door Hyundai Accent squeezed snugly in between late model SUVs, and the neighbourhood dogs even had their own park! In Redfern *every* park was a dog park, whether the sign prohibited dogs or not. Dogs shat in the street, they shat in the parks—maybe even the odd resident shat in the street too. In Coogee rubbish was recycled; in Redfern bins overflowed with paper and bottles—mostly bottles—and the rest tumbled on to the street alongside the odd syringe.

I was still smiling at the distant joggers when abruptly, alarm was in the air, just as it is when a shark is sighted near shore: a man, shouting wildly, looking my way, clasped his head in horror, covering his eyes; another man was sprinting full tilt from a far corner. I saw Jia-Mei's ball bumbling in the breeze. A massive dog hurtled towards it, its ears flying in the wind, muscles glistening as they flexed, and with each huge stride saliva sprayed from its lolloping tongue as it galloped full speed towards my tiny, frail child.

'Jia-Mei!' I screamed, already in full flight, protective fear propelling me faster than I thought possible. I closed my eyes as the thud of the impact crunched in my ears and sent her up, flying and then sprawling on the turf like a rag doll in her purple woolly dressing-gown. The sprinting man was closing in, yelling the dog's name as I reached my crumpled child. Jia-Mei had scrambled up and was staring at the dog's nose that poked down into her face, sniffing.

'I'm so sorry,' said the man, grabbing his monster by the collar. 'I'm so sorry, is she hurt, is she okay? Are you okay?'

'She's fine,' I said, relieved.

'He wouldn't hurt her, I didn't . . .'

'Hey, it was an accident, she's fine,' I said more to myself than to him. I was amazed. She wasn't even crying. Instead, with a little 'Bah', she was poking her nose back at the dog, who towered over her like a Herculean giant.

'You have the most amazing little girl,' the man said, hands shaking, putting his dog on a lead. 'She's not even frightened.'

'I know,' I said as pride and love swelled within me.

'I've never seen anything like it,' he continued. 'All children run from this dog. She's fearless, I've never seen anything like it, she's amazing.'

At this point Magnus ventured nearby and started up with his croaky, little yelp. The Great Dane turned his way, tensed his muscles, and softly growled from the back of his throat in warning. Magnus hurriedly pissed on a tuft of grass and scuttled back to the safety of the bushes as the colossal Great Dane turned back to his new friend, who was now patting him.

Somehow Jia-Mei made everyone shine. You could see it on the faces of our visitors and the shopkeepers at Randwick Plaza. Yes, she was calm and contained wherever we went, she never grabbed at things like other children, she never screamed, just stood by patiently holding our hands. She stared at the world, taking it all in with the calm of a Buddhist monk. I think it was this last thing that infected everyone with peace and generosity—she was a living, breathing spiritual icon that brought out the best in everyone, or so it seemed to her proud parents.

I recall buying her some chips in McDonald's at Randwick Plaza just before her second birthday. The whole time she was there, Jia-Mei just obediently stayed on the seat, didn't utter a sound, and ate her food quietly. A Chinese man was sitting near us, and as he got up to leave, he patted Jia-Mei on the head without saying a word, but on his face was a smile I'll never forget. 'This is how we produce children in China,' it seemed to say, 'you are lucky to have a child like this and not one of those Western children who scream and carry on.'

Everyone reacted similarly. 'What a gem! You've got a bottler there!' they cried. 'She's so intelligent,' some said. 'Look at her eyes, she's deeply thinking about everything she sees and processing it.'

Even our new social worker, Susan (pseudonym), on the

first of two post-placement visits, thought she was special. 'God she's good,' she proclaimed after Jia-Mei had sat quietly on the floor for the full two hours with a little pile of toys, never once interrupting. Experience had told Susan she'd have Buckley's chance of getting through the interview with an insecure toddler hovering in the wings.

As the session concluded Jia-Mei came over and clambered onto Susan's lap. 'She's a remarkable child, but she doesn't want to be doing this in six months time,' she said. For Susan such lack of discrimination, choosing the stranger over the parent, indicated an attachment disorder she didn't want to see on her next visit.

'Well that's a bit threatening, isn't it?' Sharon said as she closed the front door. 'What if she *is* doing this in six months time? You can't make her close to you, can you?'

'Perhaps you need to spend more time with her,' I said as Sharon climbed the stairs on her way back to her computer.

'I *do* spend time with her,' she said as she reached the top of the stairs.

'Perhaps you need to spend some full days. With all this work on, it's only mornings or afternoons—you've never spent a complete day with her.'

'Stuart, I have to get this script finished before your leave is used up. After that I'll be spending every day with her.' And with that, she was gone.

It was perplexing. Sharon was a fabulous mother, nurturing and caring. But the Sharon I knew was exuberance personified. Where was the devil-may-care? Where was the spark that lit up entire gatherings with wicked fun? Why wasn't she showering Jia-Mei with her laughter and zest for life? Where was that spirit which declaimed: 'Oh give me a great love or I shall die'?

'She hasn't bonded,' whispered Jia-Mei's godmother, Amy, a

family friend who happened to be Chinese, as she looked at Sharon and Jia-Mei together in the yard through the back window the next day. I said nothing but I knew she was right.

'Don't you think it's odd she never smiles?' Sharon posed over dinner after Amy left. For me Jia-Mei was the quintessential orphan. She didn't react, she didn't smile, she would take time to bond.

'It'll come good in time, Sharon, it's all there, simmering under the surface, waiting to come out. Look, she didn't say boo when we started, now she's babbling like a chimpanzee.'

You never know how much you love someone until they're gone, or almost gone. It was a Saturday evening two weeks later and Sharon was on the phone to one of her many friends. Jia-Mei was pottering in the yard with me, but must have wandered back into the house. As I took in the night sky and ripped the top off a beer, I heard a commotion inside. Sharon was racing up the hall carrying Jia-Mei, who was gurgling and foaming at the mouth and shrieking in terror. 'Stuart!' Sharon yelled, thrusting our child at me.

'What is it?' I screamed, hurling my bottle into the garden, paralysed with fear.

'She's got a sweet . . . she's choking, she's choking, I can't get it out, I can't get it out. She can't breathe, Stuart, I can't get it out!' yelled Sharon. 'Do something!'

No longer screaming, Jia-Mei was struggling for breath; panic seared in her eyes and she was turning blue.

'Jesus!' I yelled, taking her from Sharon. I had no idea what to do so I stuck my fingers down her throat.

'What're you doing, for Christ's sake? You're making it worse!' screamed Sharon.

It had been over two minutes and we knew if our child didn't get breath soon ... Like an idiot I panicked and lifted her upside down by the ankles, trying to shake the offending object free, all the while hitting her on the chest.

'Not like that!' Sharon shrieked as she righted Jia-Mei with one arm and pushed me to the ground with the other. It was a race against time. Where it came from, neither of us knew, but as Sharon grabbed our choking daughter instinct took over. Draping Jia-Mei over my knees we both began to pound her back, unable to breathe ourselves, watching in horror as our child went listless, eyes bulging and rolling back in her head.

'Get the car,' I shouted just as the red lolly popped out and stuck fast to the tiled floor.

Sharon took Jia-Mei in her arms and comforted her as she wailed from the shock. 'Mama,' Jia-Mei cried, 'Mama.'

'I love you, little one, oh I love you,' Sharon soothed as tears of relief tumbled down her cheeks.

'We could have been organising a funeral tonight,' murmured Sharon, still ashen-faced as she came down the stairs after tucking our child up in bed.

'I know,' I said, still shaken myself. But one thing became clear that day, even to Sharon herself: if she'd ever had attachment issues with Jia-Mei she never would again.

Four months after we returned from China it was Jia-Mei's birthday and Batch 13 turned up in grand style. The children were resplendent in their Pumpkin Patch Sunday bests and ecstatic with the thrill of a party in the air. It was a landmark day with our children now solidly entrenched with us—a day that really marked the beginning of our journey forward with them, a day to remember.

Rarely has an entire ensemble been as happy as we all were that day. Everyone was keen to tell their story and learn how the rest of the batch had been faring. But as we all spoke excitedly over the top of each other our eyes kept drifting back to the children.

Our yard had turned into a playground. Sharon, who remember had vowed to never spoil the child, had already set Jia-Mei up with all manner of bikes and scooters, countless dolls, dolly cots and strollers and a playpen stuffed to overflowing.

Although only two, Jia-Mei knew the day was all about her and she thrived in the spotlight. The other children tried to get in on the act as she unwrapped her presents, but she elbowed them out of the way as she grappled with boxes that were sometimes bigger than herself. On her head sat a little yellow hat that my daughter Jo had given her. Just like her mother, Jia-Mei wore a hat at every opportunity.

Champagne corks popped and the wine and beer flowed. Alec in particular was ebullient and the jokes flew fast and furious. 'Look at them,' he said as we all once again stared at our four tiny babies in wonder. 'What else do you need in life?' he shouted to us all, swept away, raising his wine glass.

'To our beautiful children!' proposed another, and a cheer went up accompanying this impromptu toast.

Then all eyes turned to Alec, sensing there was more to come: 'You can't buy this!' he proclaimed in exultation, face beaming, eyes twinkling.

Everyone smiled and nodded and cheered more loudly than before as Sharon, always out for a laugh, yelled above them all: 'We *did* buy this!'

For a moment there was stunned silence. No-one moved a muscle. But as the group digested the irony of the twenty thousand dollars it had cost to adopt, the laughter began. 'How could you say such a thing in front of the girls!' Pru reprimanded, but the laughter swamped her protest and built until it climaxed in a mighty tumult.

CHAPTER 10

WHERE ARE YOU GOING, MY LITTLE ONE?

Sharon

For the past hour my eyes had been fixed on the garage waiting for Stuart to come home from work. When the electronic door opened it took all my energy not to bail him up there and then.

'Dada,' squealed Jia-Mei from her highchair, arms extended. Putting his bag down, Stuart picked her up and covered her food-smeared face with kisses. As he turned to me my pent-up anxiety and panic tumbled out. 'Something's wrong! Terribly wrong! Jia-Mei's eyes aren't inquisitive, she ignores me when I speak to her—it's all wrong! Even a day-old monkey holds on . . .' I said finally, looking at Jia-Mei's arms and legs dangling from Stuart's body.

Gently putting our little daughter down, Stuart took off his coat as if trying to work out how to deal with this. His responses can take an eternity but when they finally flow, there is real sense to them.

'Withdrawn, not responding to stimulus, not smiling—it's all consistent with adoption trauma,' he said, taking off his shoes.

'It's not adoption trauma!' I wailed. 'It's more, it's in the eyes!' Looking at my darling daughter I tried to suppress the deep fear gripping my body.

Jia-Mei, chubby legs extended on the floor, was pawing a page in her food book with a voracious gaze. Slowly her little lips protruded like a chimpanzee's about to peel a banana. ''range,' she squeaked.

Stuart recited tales from the books he'd read on adopting a child from overseas. 'The real child doesn't emerge until double the adoption age,' he said. 'If you still feel this way when she's just over three then I might be concerned, but she's still a baby—and God knows what went on with the foster mother.'

Our fondness for Jia-Mei's foster mother had waned. In China, when she told us Jia-Mei spent most of the day in her cot, it had struck us as odd. With us she lay silently awake in her cot for hours until you took her out. We decided she never cried because her cries had always gone unanswered.

'Bloody foster mother!' I fumed.

We both smiled at Jia-Mei, who was testing the edibility of food pages and giving them to Magnus to see if he wanted a bite.

Stuart, as he always does, erased my fear. What was I thinking? How could anything be wrong? 'She's so bright,' said everyone: her Chinese godmother, my brother, friends with grown-up children. The voices were unanimous: we had hit the jackpot. 'Look at the way she sits in her highchair for hours without demanding attention.'; 'Look at the way she holds her pencil.'; 'She's an extraordinary child!'

Jia-Mei was extraordinary, they were right. She slept well, never cried, ate everything and stole the hearts of all.

'I can't believe it got to you,' I said, opening the back door to let in the spring scent of jasmine. Stuart, sitting at the dining-room table, was staring in amazement at a letter in his hand addressed to: 'Neal Stuart, ABC, Australia.'

I had just returned from the zoo with Jia-Mei when I checked the letterbox. Along with the letter in Mandarin were laminated photos of the foster mother and her daughter. 'Jia-Mei, look what Mummy's got!' I said excitedly as she eyed me cautiously. She was still getting used to her exuberant new mother. Intrigued to see her reaction, I watched closely as I put them in her tiny hands. Instead of recoiling in horror as I believed she may, her face lit up.

'Oh!' she exclaimed in delight, a massive smile lighting her face. She looked at the photos and me in wonder, kissing them, clutching them and staring at her foster mother's face as if willing it to come alive. It brought tears to my eyes and shame to my heart. We'd certainly been too quick to point the bone.

Leaving her poring over the faces, the letter was immediately faxed to Jia-Mei's Chinese godmother, who translated it and sent it back.

Reading the letter now, Stuart too was moved. It was from someone sick with worry, someone who had nurtured our baby with love: 'She didn't sleep well, waking up and crying. So that my husband and daughter's sleep was not disrupted I often had to cradle Mei Mei and slept on the sofa with her.'

The letter showed a desperate need for assurance that Jia-Mei now had a good loving home. She told us how 'Mei Mei' had been very sick when she got her at just over two months old.

She'd had continual dysentery and cried night and day, either because she was not well or was undernourished. She had been very thin, her hair patchy and wiry, her complexion yellowish—but after a few months, with love and care, the tiny child had flourished and had gradually learnt to smile. 'If she has problems with responses, please be a little patient,' she wrote. 'Mei Mei is an intelligent child, she will learn to be obedient and bring you joy and happiness.' And finally: 'Should this letter get to you, I hope you will reply to it.'

It had been sent three months after we adopted Jia-Mei. Foster carers are strictly told not to contact adoptive families, yet this woman had done what most Chinese don't dare—defy the authorities. I wrote straight back, delighted to assuage her fears.

'The happiest years of my life were when youse were all around my feet,' my mother would lament to me constantly when I was a teenager in her thick brogue, 'but I didn't know it, Sharon.' Then her deep, strong voice burst forth as she followed me around the room staring into my eyes, singing the same song that inevitably left her awash with tears:

> *Where are you going*
> *My little one, little one?*
> *Where are you going*
> *My baby, my own?*

> *Turn around and you're two*
> *Turn around and you're four*
> *Turn around and you're a young girl*
> *Going out of the door.*

She was a card, my old mum, and because of her brainwashing I cherished every minute of Jia-Mei's early days in Australia. Between Wiggles concerts, going to the zoo with Batch 13, to playgrounds, to the beach and our first Carols by Candlelight. We had a ball together.

Weekends were precious. Every Saturday morning Jia-Mei would eat the toast Stuart had made as she sat rapt in the musical gyrations of urgent, half-dressed pop singers on *Video Hits*. Sometimes she would lie between us as we read the papers, pretending to read as well with her book invariably upside down. Other times, as the sun shone through the bedroom slats, we would just stare at her in awe and bask in the rays of family life.

'Bye,' she waved as Stuart ushered her upstairs, his protective arms shadowing her wobbling ascent. With her mop of hair, tiny, sturdy squat body, little gremlin nose and dark solemn eyes ringed by thick tufts of fringe, she still reminded me of the little woodland creature we'd bought in Hong Kong. And, as she reached the top of the stairs, a Sunday evening back in October vividly flashed through my mind.

Jia-Mei had always spurned touch. Like a timid animal she didn't want a bar of it and I knew I had to tread slowly. I started by strategically placing my foot on a rung of her highchair beneath her own. At other times my arm crept close while she watched TV. Eventually these actions became habit. So on this Sunday night I crouched, waiting for her to fall asleep, my face close to the cot, my hand next to her body. Her black hair was longer, her normally furrowed brow relaxed; her face soft. My urchin duckling was transforming into a swan. Lost in my thoughts I hadn't noticed she'd clasped my finger until she squeezed. It was the first bit of affection she'd ever shown and my vision blurred with tears. We stayed like that until she fell asleep. As I gazed at her in slumber I realised I loved this child more deeply than I could ever have imagined and that she loved me too. The unseen string of energy that lives on its own between two people that I call true love was finally there and would never be broken.

'Aroooooo!' howled Stuart from upstairs, breaking my reverie. 'Aroooo,' he howled again, setting the neighbour's dog off. Magnus was scratching desperately at the back door with his own croaky bark. 'Ro, ro, ro,' went Stuart. Amidst all the noise another sound echoed downstairs, rooting me to the spot. Jia-Mei was in fits of giggles. Moving up the stairs, I started to giggle myself. 'Yip, yip, yip,' Stuart enthused, and again peels of giggles ripped through the house, followed by choking-for-breath guffaws. Now I was listening outside the bedroom door, terrified of breaking the moment and bathing in the music of our child's hysterical mirth.

'My God!' I exclaimed to Stuart when he finally came out of the room.

'I know,' he said looking shocked, clutching the magical Hairy Maclary book in his hands. 'See, I told you it was only a matter of time.'

Every January for the past three years Stuart and I had attended the two-week Tamworth Country Music Festival. Jia-Mei loved music and we were thrilled to be taking her with us this time.

'Jolene, Jolene, Jolene, Jolene . . .' warbled the busker sweating heavily from the overwhelming heat to the constantly moving throng decked out in akubras and cowboy gear. For a small town, Tamworth has more pubs and clubs than either of us has ever seen and during the festival they are alive with quality bands. Morning and night you are surrounded by music.

An ever-changing string of buskers lines the streets and mall: male, female, duets and Von-Trapp type families with children as young as three—every aspiring musician has a go. Drink abounds but the crowd's essence is simply unified in a generosity of spirit and the desire for a bloody good time.

But we were nonplussed by Jia-Mei's response to Tamworth. Either she wasn't a country music fan or something else was at play. She'd also stopped laughing at Hairy Maclary and no other book elicited so much as a smile. 'She's unpredictable this little one,' we agreed, wondering if the crowds had overwhelmed her. Even the fairground got a tepid response. We had been there four days and this was our last night.

The sun descended quickly and in the gloom we approached our car parked alongside the multicoloured, flickering fairground. Jia-Mei, who had been bobbing half asleep on Stuart's shoulders, sat bolt upright. 'Dada,' she squealed pointing, desperate to get down. Instead of running towards the whirling noise of the fairground she bolted towards an old man busking on the side of the street, hardly visible in the evening's hue. The old man's hands were gnarled and his akubra, torn and stained, had seen better days. Others walked past without a glance, ignoring his desperate and heartfelt attempts to compete against the blaring pop songs of the fairground.

Our curious child stood staring at the man's dusty, weather-beaten face, captivated. 'Down came the troopers, one, two, three!' Then as if someone had wound her up, she started to dance. Up and down she bounced, swaying from side to side amidst little skips that sent her tottering. Regaining herself, she started again and with arms flapping in between little claps of joy she turned, whirling around and around. The old man's eyes locked on Jia-Mei and stooping low, half-bemused, he increased

the intensity of his voice, inciting her into frenzy: 'Waltzing Matilda, waltzing Matilda . . .'

It was a strange moment. What had ignited her? Singers had
abounded, yet she had shown no interest. At dusk, under the
street lamp with the old man playing his guitar and the little
Chinese baby dancing in her cowboy hat, I was reminded of
figurines on a musical box—two lonely souls lost in the music.
When it was over Jia-Mei clapped vigorously, bellowing, 'Bah'
over and over. The man could only nod, bewildered by this curious, beguiling child whose spark his music had ignited deep
within. As we walked away I turned. The old man was staring
after us and he continued to stare until we were out of sight.

CHAPTER 11

ONE HORROR STORY TOO MANY

Sharon

When we returned that January we set about hurrying DoCS into processing our application for Jia-Mei's sister. With all the hurdles such children face—adoption, different culture, older parents—we knew we had to adopt two, so they would have each other to share their differences, even if they didn't get on. All the literature pointed to this being a surer path to a well-adjusted childhood.

The 12-month wait was now nearly up and we were determined this time that as soon as we were eligible we would push them. We had learnt through a Batch 13 mate that such pushing got her through the system a year faster than us; we would be relentless this time.

January 2005 was also memorable for another reason. It was when all the odd things started to happen.

I had started writing a psychological horror story based

on events related to me by a social worker friend in the United Kingdom, Esther (pseudonym). She had been case-managing a ten-year-old child accused of setting up her young friend for a pack rape. When Esther first met the child before the case started she was astonished. The young girl, Solange (pseudonym), had impeccable manners, was sophisticated, sweet and innocent.

Esther had many years experience dealing with sexual offences involving young children. The charges against Solange simply didn't make sense. Her colleagues agreed, as did three leading psychiatrists, whose reports were unanimous: Solange was not capable of such a crime. It was Solange's word against the other girl's and the prosecution case was weak.

However, returning one afternoon from court with Solange beside her in the car, there was an incident that left Esther shaking. 'I was concentrating on the motorway,' she told me, 'and curiously, now having listened to Solange's "friend" testify in court, I was really unsure about who was telling the truth. At the very moment I thought this, I could feel Solange looking at me. There was a weird energy and I could feel myself choking. I glanced at Solange and her face looked different, it was like . . . the shape . . . the whole face looked like someone else's, it looked like other eyes were staring out. Suddenly she said, in a voice which wasn't hers—deep, like a man's: "You're wondering if I did it, aren't you? Well I did!" The child then started to laugh, but it wasn't the laugh of a child. I almost swerved off the road and when I turned to her she looked normal again, she had no recollection at all.'

Although freaked out, Esther, being a rational person, believed she was tired, her mind playing tricks. But she couldn't shake it and eventually, expecting to be laughed out of the room, related her experience to a colleague. Instead of incredulity, the colleague's response shocked her. She too had experienced an 'incident' and thought she had imagined it. So was it in both their minds, or was it a supernatural event? Esther believed strongly that such things were not possible.

Being Irish and a sucker for ghost stories, it got me thinking and I started writing about a woman battling with her sanity. Were the strange events involving the ten-year-old child in her care real or imagined?

Only able to write late at night, I found myself jumping at shadows as I became swept up by the story, and shook my head at the silliness of it. Only later did I realise that it was around this time that my little Jia-Mei with the dark, searching eyes had gone silent. Sometime during this period she stopped babbling, but I hadn't yet put my finger on what was going on. Indeed, when I think back on it, it was hard to get any sound out of her at all.

I must have sensed something was amiss though—it's all still so vivid—because during the days I spent every ounce of energy trying to get interaction from my little girl. Then at night, exhausted, I sat at my computer and frightened the living daylights out of myself writing about burial grounds, insect infestations and psychological disturbance with my own mind fuelled by a disquiet that I couldn't pin down. I have a lively imagination at the best of times—but it was as if life started to mirror art when odd things began to happen in the house.

'Bloody hell!' shouted Stuart downstairs from the kitchen one Saturday morning in February. As I came racing down the stairs, fearing something had happened to Jia-Mei, I saw him vacuuming the kitchen, which was alive with crawling maggots. We'd both lived in fairly dingy shared accommodation when we were young, but neither of us had experienced maggots. They covered the floor, writhing and squirming. I was horrified. Every time he vacuumed, more came. 'I can't work out where they are they coming from,' he puzzled. It seemed to be all parts of the kitchen. When we finally thought they'd all gone, we'd spy another little bugger wriggling from a crevice.

The pest controller was promptly called in. They weren't maggots, they were moth larvae. The entire house was sprayed, including the cupboards, and every bit of food was sealed in plastic bags.

'It's impossible,' he said over the phone when I told him they had come back a week later. He blasted them again, but once more they came back, writhing over the floor like they owned the bloody place. After three weeks of it I'd had enough: the house was going on the market.

Stuart interrupted my ranting: 'Shit, look at that!'

The vertical blinds that covered our massive sliding doors were covered in flies. There were hundreds of them hovering and buzzing in massed packs.

I was now convinced the house was built on bad land. As the day progressed it became an Aboriginal burial ground I'd read about in the research for my script that was now scaring the pants off me.

I got a grip and calmed down, and after a week or so the flies and maggots seemed to have vacated and gone to insect heaven in a swathe of pesticide.

Then in April my computer crashed. I lost the entire script that had been haunting my waking thoughts. 'It's the weirdest thing,' said the technician. Neither he nor his colleagues had ever encountered a hard disk and a back-up disk failing at the same time, let alone completely wiping all data. 'I can't explain it,' he said. 'You must have a poltergeist because in my experience it's not possible.'

Right!

By May Jia-Mei was in her own bedroom, and although I hadn't overtly noticed my little girl's silent demeanour, I'm sure instinctually I had picked it up. Each morning I went to her cot to find her unnaturally quiet, lying there silently waiting for me. Her dark, haunted eyes, devoid of animation or smile, would watch me intently as if she was sizing things up. 'She has a most unusual quality,' people would murmur, 'she looks at you like she's reading your mind.' At other times: 'There's something "unreal" about Jia-Mei.' 'When she looks at you it's not like the eyes of a child. It's like she's been here many times before.'; 'She has the eyes of an old soul.'; 'Look, the way she holds that pen, it's way beyond her years.'; 'It's like she senses things in people; don't you notice how she'll only go to some people?' It seemed everyone was saying the same thing: my little girl was deeply intelligent, enigmatic and very unusual.

But no-one could quite work out anything clearly about Jia-Mei. Around this time a Chinese international student visited to meet her. Pru also came over with her little girl. As mothers hungry to learn about our children's culture we pounded the student with questions. Could she tell anything about their possible backgrounds by looking at them? Pru's child, she said, looked like all Chinese children. Jia-Mei, however, looked quite different, unlike any child she'd seen. I knew Jia-Mei may have come from a minority ethnic group and proposed this. She shook her head as if something was swimming in her mind that she couldn't quite gather in.

This mysterious response encouraged my growing belief that Jia-Mei was truly special, different, perhaps she would grow up to be a sage. Pulling my Irish heritage close I blossomed with pride. She would be fey, I was sure. She had the 'touch'. It also further gave me the spooks.

That very evening I went to see a movie called *The Grudge* with Jia-Mei's favourite person, Barry, an actor friend. Based on a Japanese film, *The Grudge* was a straight-out horror movie involving a dead child at the top of the stairs in an old, run-down house. The child, around seven, peered from the balcony motionless, silently watching with dark, haunting eyes and an umbrella of thick, black hair.

'That girl remind you of anyone?' Barry laughed as we left the cinema. There was no question about it. The dead soul looked just as Jia-Mei did when she lay in our bed and stared at us for hours without moving; her calm, composed eyes framed by a riot of thick, black hair.

My fertile mind was wild with imaginings. Stuart was headed for a book fair in New York and as the time approached I was jumpy and truly beginning to freak out. Half-joking one evening over a glass of wine, I said to a close girlfriend that often, walking up the stairs late at night, I expected to hear a deep guttural voice coming from Jia-Mei's room: 'I'm watching you.' I laughed at the absurdity of it. My friend did not.

'I know what you mean,' she said. She often felt spooked by Jia-Mei's demeanour.

Irish ghost stories had been part of my night-time routine as a child. My mother loved telling them and I loved hearing them. I can see now that the impetus to write a story about illusion and reality sprang from swirling fears in my subconscious. But I couldn't shake what others didn't see: there was something wrong with my baby.

Amy, Jia-Mei's Chinese godmother, had said a while back I hadn't bonded with my child. That really surprised me at the time as I loved her without doubt. But somehow I was troubled: she was too remote, too detached.

'Children are funny,' a friend had laughed the evening before we picked Jia-Mei up in China; 'the things they say and do are hilarious.' But Jia-Mei didn't really do anything. When we put her on the floor, she stayed put. When we tickled her she stared, mute. It confused me that, even after all this time, I couldn't get a handle on her personality.

'How's yours going?' I'd ask American Beth from Batch 13, hanging off her every word. She had no problem rattling out character traits and idiosyncrasies. 'Jia-Mei's kind and compliant,' was all I could come up with.

I'd never had a child so didn't know what to expect. 'All children develop differently,' our DoCS social worker had barked when I asked why Jia-Mei wasn't speaking. She, who had experience, didn't think it was odd, so why did I? What did I see that they didn't? And why did I have this question that wouldn't go away: is she normal?

By October, as Stuart set off to Frankfurt for yet another book fair, Jia-Mei appeared increasingly different to other children. My inner confusion was fuelled when I attended a party at Jia-Mei's Family Day Carer's house. Family Day Care, which took place in the carer's home with just a handful of children, was a preferable child-care option for us over the large, day-care-centre model. Watching her among the five other children sent my heart pounding; she wasn't interacting like them. Blind Freddy could see it! Why hadn't the Family Day Carer said anything? In panic, I contacted the Family Day Care scheme's director. The following week they sent someone to observe and assess Jia-Mei. The person, a qualified child care worker, reported Jia-Mei was an intelligent normal little girl.

Was it all in my mind then? More and more I began to feel like the protagonist in my script.

Time and time again I would query Beth from Batch 13 about her child's responses and speech, trying to get a gauge. Jia-Mei sometimes reminded me of a cat who would turn when you called and then ignore you at other times.

'Get her ears checked,' Beth urged, 'she could have glue ear.' I'd never heard of such a thing but was sure Jia-Mei heard fine. Beth is a quietly forceful person and for that I am grateful because finally her pushing got us to the doctor's surgery. Jia-Mei indeed had the thing I'd never heard of: water in the ear, a condition known as glue ear that can make children unresponsive, slow to speak and detached.

I was euphoric with relief. There was a reason. I hadn't imagined it. My poor, poor little baby!

The operation went smoothly and there was a marked difference immediately. Jia-Mei was more vocal, more lively, more alert—and for the first time she was spontaneously smiling.

CHAPTER 12

PUPPETS AND TEARS

Stuart

Friday, 29 July was a cool, clear, winter's day in Sydney; the sort of day where there's still plenty of warmth in the sun but if cloud comes over it's another story.

'Stuart, Stuart, Stuart!' Sharon screamed from upstairs. It was the day our adoption of a second child turned from dream to reality. Miracle of miracles! We had been approved with lightning speed, a mere four months since applying.

That very same day, Jia-Mei was due to have her grommets checked; these had been inserted in her ears to treat her glue ear. I had to work, but at 2.45 p.m., half an hour before the appointment, I found myself in the car chugging down Anzac Parade on my way to join Sharon and Jia-Mei. Sharon beamed with uninhibited joy as I walked into Dr McDonald's (pseudonym) surgery. She wasn't expecting me and neither was Jia-Mei. 'Dada, Dada, Dada,' she called out excitedly as I picked her up and held her high over my head before sitting and placing her on my lap.

'You wouldn't be dead for quids,' I thought.

Dr McDonald was gentle and caring, a real humanitarian. The grommets were draining the fluid; the operation had been a success. 'You'll be talking in no time, little one,' he said, smiling at Jia-Mei as he shepherded us towards the audiologist's room for the routine hearing test.

'There's a nifty way to assess people's hearing when they're little and don't have language,' the audiologist explained sunnily. 'When a sound is played a brightly lit puppet jumps up suddenly. The child soon associates sound with the puppet. After she gets the hang of it we distract her with toys and play more sounds. If she hears a sound she'll turn to the puppet's dark box and be rewarded with it springing to life in dazzling light. If she doesn't turn she hasn't heard it. In this way we can map what sounds she hears.' We knew Jia-Mei could hear and nodded affably.

The small room, like a cinema, had just enough light to see. Jia-Mei was strategically placed and latched on to the game straight away. A foghorn boomed, she turned to the box, up the puppet sprang, and the audiologist marked her grid. I wanted to applaud. All sorts of sounds came out and time and again she turned to the puppet. Sharon looked my way and rolled her eyes with characteristic impatience as if to say 'get on with it, this is unbelievably boring. We're going to have a second child, we've finally got the family we've always wanted, let's get home and celebrate!' But beneath this I knew she was as attentive as a hawk.

The noises kept coming and the audiologist kept marking her grid. There were sounds I could barely hear myself, in fact I'm not sure I didn't miss a few. I noticed Jia-Mei didn't get a couple of the very faint, high ones, but why would she when she was engrossed in a pile of brand-new toys? Then I jumped with a start and teetered on the edge of my seat. How could she not hear that one? But I relaxed when I checked out her brow furrowed in deep concentration, carefully stacking blocks. No, she's still engrossed in the game, she's alright. Or was she? Why was I still clinging to the edge of my seat, leaning as far forward as possible?

Then a long, clear, high pitch, a bit like the sound the TV makes when normal transmission has ceased, rang through the air. A shiver ran up my spine and my heart started to pound as I stared and stared at my little girl's back: 'Turn around, baby, turn around, oh please, please, please . . .' I didn't need the audiologist to say it. Sharon's stiff body had told me long before what I didn't want to know. Sharon had picked it as soon as the high sounds started; she had long since stopped moving, her eyes fixed in shock and fierce protection as she stared at our child: our little girl who was deaf.

It's a sad fact about me that while I understand lots of things, sometimes of great complexity, too often when something's staring me in the face I can't see it. Or I won't allow myself to see it, I'm never sure which. Sharon on the other hand never misses a trick. I am sure she knew before the audiologist knew.

The test was over and we were back in the bright lights. Just like that there was talk of The Shepherd Centre for deaf children and how hearing aids come in unobtrusive colours. 'It's government funded, won't cost you anything,' said the audiologist, as if it was good news.

Dr McDonald was devastated that he'd misdiagnosed the situation. His compassion for our little girl, who'd already been through so much, was tearing him apart. Jia-Mei had mild to moderate hearing loss in the high frequencies. 'She can't hear consonants like "s", "p", "f" and "t". Hearing aids are essential, but with the early intervention of speech therapy she should be able to start school and catch up with the others,' he said brightly, but his eyes remained sad. My mind whirled. When I said 'stop', she heard 'o'; when we said 'sit' she heard 'i'; no wonder the poor little thing's speech wasn't forthcoming. No-one looking on saw any change in my demeanour. That's the way it is with me.

Making the next appointment of many, I saw an ashen Sharon shaking hands with an equally ashen Dr McDonald, and then in a poignant moment he knelt down to our child who was smiling up from her stroller. 'I guess you and I will grow old together Jia-Mei,' he said softly with a tragic smile.

Sharon was fiercely protective of Jia-Mei that evening and fed her and bathed her with intimate care. She put her to bed with soothing lullabies. Afterwards we sat at the table for a drink with Jo, my 20-year-old daughter, but it wasn't to toast anything as planned.

The following Sunday, 31 July, we celebrated Jia-Mei's birthday a day early. Our Batch 13 friends poured in joyously, chatting excitedly, picking up children and twirling them around and around in circles, popping champagne corks, photographing anything that moved and embracing whoever was nearby. The kids were excited too, chasing each other all over the yard and through the house.

But in a far lonely corner, out of the way, our little girl crept from all, her face stricken with a distress that tore my heart. 'She knows she's different. I just wish they would all go,' Sharon whispered in a voice cracked with emotion as she stared at Jia-Mei hunched over, drawing, her back to the party as if trying to escape into the paper in front of her.

As Jia-Mei withdrew the other children played on oblivious,

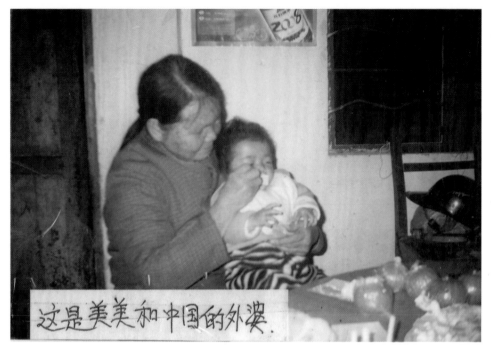

这是美美和中国的外婆.

The earliest photo we have of Jessie Mei Mei (Jia-Mei), around seven months. She is being fed by her foster grandmother.

Jessie Mei Mei (Jia-Mei) in a park in Nanning, China, around 13 months.

'This'll do, right here. Jia-Mei won't know where she came from anyway and her mother could be from anywhere. Let's just take some photos now and be done with it,' cried Sharon. In the end Kylie's excited face won the day and we ploughed on and punted across the river.

While this finding site is of no account to anyone but us, the brutal, cement steps of the building where a desperate mother left her newborn to the mercy of others, is the unprepossessing scene of great human tragedy.

The tiny village where Jessie Mei Mei (Jia-Mei) was left by her birth mother. No luxuries or fancy cars in this world despite the twelve-lane super-highway which threatened like a predator just metres away.

The morning we became parents. Jessie Mei Mei (Jia-Mei) clutching her woodland creature sucks in the big ones in between screaming bouts.

Jessie Mei Mei (Jia-Mei), a traumatised rag doll at the steps of her orphanage where there was no-one there to meet us. Not so for the excited others who are just out of shot as Sharon looks on.

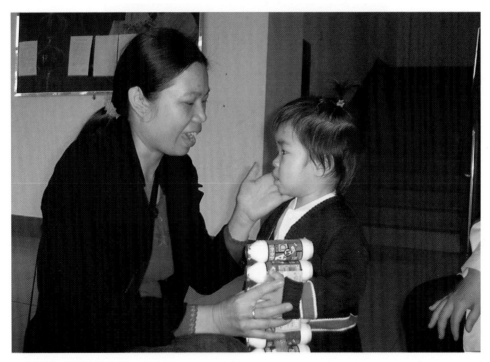

Jessie Mei Mei's (Jia-Mei's) foster mother tore across town to see the baby she had nurtured for 18 months, one last time. She holds back the tears as she passes her parting gift of little milks.

Jessie Mei Mei (Jia-Mei), nearly two, with her Mama at a Batch 13 gathering.

A rare moment of giggles as Dada reads a story.

'I tell you, if you leave her on this drug she'll die!' screamed Sharon to no effect.
Here Jessie Mei Mei battles the cumulative effect of the controversial anti-psychotic,
Risperidone. To leave her like this for another three and a half months was unconscionable.

Yang Mei-Bi (Bi Bi) desperately unhappy in the orphanage environment . . . 'almost all
were rocking from one foot to the other, swaying rhythmically like long grass on a gusty
headland'.

So desperate for touch—Bi Bi's orphanage, Yangjiang, China.

In the restaurant of the magnificent White Swan Hotel, Guangzhou, China. Our new family poses with a Chinese friend.

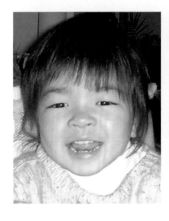

The many faces of Jessie Mei Mei.

speaking to each other in rudimentary English. Sharon, the proud mother, had organised the party of parties with games and songs and presents for all. Valiantly she tried with effervescent yet gentle encouragement to coax our little girl into its midst. When she realised that Jia-Mei just didn't want to know, I could see all she wanted to do was end the day there and then. But you can't pull the plug on a whole load of excited parents and three-year-old children, so she played the hostess with eyes rarely straying from the tiny back in the corner of the room.

The anguish on Sharon's face was plain as she bit into her trembling bottom lip and it broke my heart. The image of her bravely battling tears, face scrunched in torture as she courageously tried to keep it painted with a smile still haunts me to this day.

For Jia-Mei it was as if our sadness had infected her, even though we had gone out of our way to keep things bright and bubbly. She looked to be affected by grief in a way only adults can be. But there was more to it than that, and it was all over Sharon's face. Our child was overwhelmed. She couldn't cope because the other children were now so much more competent than she. She couldn't cope because she couldn't grasp anything. She couldn't cope because she was deaf and all around her was cacophony and mayhem.

The next day neither of us went to work. The phone rang downstairs but we didn't answer it. It was Dr McDonald. He left a heartfelt message. 'I couldn't stop thinking about Jia-Mei all weekend,' he said, his compassionate voice cracked with emotion.

Sharon and I loved the name Jia-Mei (which we later learnt was pronounced Jiow-May). We'd given her the Western name 'Jessie' too, but this was just parked away as a middle name in case she needed it one day. But somehow Jia-Mei didn't seem quite right anymore. Maybe it was the way she often didn't respond when she was called. Whatever the case, we sensed it wasn't working out.

'Geea-meea, Geea-meea,' boomed the receptionist in a flat drawl as we sat in the waiting room at Sydney Children's Hospital, waiting to see the leading paediatric team on Dr McDonald's advice.

'That's it,' said Sharon. 'She's got enough differences to deal with without people constantly getting her name wrong! If we call her Jessie, it's one less difference for her to worry about.'

The paediatric team saw no reason to believe that anything other than hearing loss and adoption trauma lay at the heart of Jia-Mei's slow speech. They wanted to be sure, however, so they recommended we attend the Tumbatin Clinic adjacent to the hospital, which could do a thorough analysis of any developmental issues. 'But there's no hurry, it's all routine.'

That afternoon we started calling Jia-Mei 'Jessie'. Down the track this morphed into 'Jessie Mei Mei'. Remarkably, she took to her new name like a duck to water, which surprised us both. Now she responded to every call. It was a miraculous transformation and with regret 'Jia-Mei' was firmly consigned to the past.

CHAPTER 13

JUST KEEP HER HAPPY

Sharon

Jessie was waking every night now—sometimes twice a night.

'Mummy's here,' I whispered, rocking her gently as I patted the mucus away from her nose. For months she'd had a chest infection. But in the warm comfort of my arms Jessie, with her book nestled close, was finally asleep. I marvelled how my distant child had grown into a desperately affectionate little girl whom I loved beyond words. Tomorrow we had an appointment with Tumbatin, the child development clinic. Now that she was making emotional progress, perhaps we could focus on a way forward with language and speech.

'Christ we're always late!' I muttered accusingly as I hurried towards the car, Jessie pulling like a mule behind me. Stuart's sardonic smile was burning my back but he knew I was anxious, and that it was me who could never get anywhere on time.

At Tumbatin we were ushered into a room and introduced

119

to the centre's psychologist, social worker and paediatric registrar. There was a stiffness to everyone's smile; under the light conversation hung the unspoken sadness that children developing normally don't come here. But while we all sat around uncomfortably, strangely Jessie was happy and compliant.

'She's so well behaved,' said the social worker.

'Beautiful,' said the young registrar. Considering she'd lately developed a hysterical aversion to all clinical environments we were as surprised as the rest of them.

'Let's go outside and have a look at her gross motor skills,' the psychologist said brightly. As usual Jessie raised the ball up to her chin with two hands and then pushed it away, in the opposite direction to the receiver. 'I love this anarchic streak,' Stuart used to say. But today we didn't laugh as we might have at home. Instead I glanced nervously at the psychologist, who kept smiling, but I knew Jessie's inability to catch or throw the ball or jump from a step really troubled her.

Back inside, Jessie had dragged one trouser leg up to her knee. It was an eccentricity that always made us smile. No matter what we put on her—footless tights or trousers—if the right leg could be dragged up to the knee, up it would go. The room looked like a playroom to Jessie and she was delighted. She charged around exploring and within a couple of seconds she was scribbling, head bent low, over some paper, propelling her little chair back and forth at a rate of knots. I caught the psychologist's beady stare. 'A lot of children from orphanages rock,' I explained glancing at Stuart, who seemed oblivious that this might be odd.

During the assessment Stuart remained with Jessie and the psychologist while the rest of us, like spies, watched the action through a one-way mirror. She started off well with the puzzles, but as the psychologist moved on to speech, imitation, imaginative play and drawing, a deep uneasy feeling settled into my being. Then Jessie made it clear she'd had enough and the last part of the test was aborted.

As we waited for the results Stuart, as usual, did his best to calm me and counter my pessimism. 'They were going to say Jessie had some problems,' he said. 'But look at her background. Prior to the fitting of her hearing aids she'd been ripped from the foster mother she loved, then thrown into the half-muted sounds of a strange language and people. Who wouldn't rock and withdraw,' he whispered, smiling and squeezing my hand reassuringly. 'And you know what?' he continued. 'She doesn't like the psychologist. She absolutely hates her. You must have noticed that. Actually I'm not that fond of her myself. You know how Jessie is when she takes a set against someone. That firm independence shows she's no fool. Why should she go along with what they want? She was happy as Larry to start with but didn't like being directed and dug her toes in. They won't take that into account. They won't understand it's about them.'

We were called in. The silence in the room was the first thing that struck me. Instinctively I pulled Jessie close.

'She has moderate global developmental delay with autistic tendencies,' announced the psychologist. I looked at Stuart, who shrugged his shoulders.

'So in time she'll catch up?' he ventured. Pitying glances were furtively exchanged. The psychologist shook her head.

'But the word *delay* means you can catch up,' continued Stuart, a pedantic word buff.

'No,' said the psychologist, somewhat irritated that we didn't get her meaning.

'But . . . but what about her adoption trauma?' asked Stuart.

'You can't hold onto that forever,' she retorted.

'So what can we do to help her?'

'Early intervention and put her into a good pre-school.'

'Anything else?' he pushed.

'Just keep her happy.'

'Keep her happy—what the friggin' hell does that mean!' I cried as we walked to the car. I was alarmed: 'happy', or else . . . what? Looking to Stuart in front for solace and support, I saw only a hunched-over figure forlornly clutching the hand of his tiny, tottering daughter. He hadn't seen it coming and was shattered.

In the car, buckling up in silence, we sat stunned as the meaning of what had been said thundered down on us. Our beautiful 3½ year old daughter was retarded. Later, over the internet, we learnt that 'moderate' is a misleading term. It actually means intellectually disabled 'big-time'. Jessie would never be able to look after herself and would only ever develop basic communication phrases.

'I still think they could have it wrong . . . if they only spent more time with her . . . they need to win her over first,' Stuart mumbled feebly.

'That's not what you think!' I broke in.

We held each other tightly for ages and kept squeezing and pulling ever closer, desperately hoping through fierce touch and sheer will our broken hearts might begin to mend.

High on a ridge, roughly in line with Tamarama Beach, Waterford Pre-school is blessed with a sense of space and calm as the land by the back fence falls steeply away, revealing the ocean in the distance. Placing a child with a disability is not easy, but after three months we cracked a placement at Waterford. We were overjoyed. Waterford had been our first choice; it's an intimate small pre-school and the staff and curriculum are second to none. The one or two children with disabilities have high support and are integrated with the other 28 'regular' children who are taught respect and warmth for difference.

I first met Fran, the disability support teacher, at Waterford's sports day. She struck me as eccentric with her high, sweet girly voice, and large straw hat adorned with flowers jutting colourfully in all directions. Fran, a devout Catholic and mother of six with flame-coloured curls and the body of a 20-year-old, was effusive but firm. A race was about to start and immediately she grabbed Jessie—who hates walking, let alone running—by the hand and buoyed her to the start. By the time Fran and Jessie got a quarter of the way up the field it was empty; the other children, having sprinted to the finish, were sitting. When finally Jessie lumbered to the end with Fran by her side the entire school erupted into a standing ovation of roaring cheers. The beam on Jessie's face will remain with me forever—as will the equally big one on Fran's. From the start Fran took no nonsense and pushed our child with a love and intensity as if she was her own. Each day she sent home a diary that showered us with positivity by detailing every little accomplishment our daughter made.

Jessie started to learn in this supportive environment. Her vocabulary began to grow and new complexity emerged in her drawing. After a couple of months Stuart was encouraged to put on a concert for the whole school just because they thought it would be good for Jessie. 'How did it go?' I asked.

'Fine,' he said.

'Just fine?'

'I think it went quite well,' he said. 'Jessie seemed pretty happy.'

Excitedly Fran painted a different picture the next day as I dropped Jessie off. Stuart had rattled through his now well-worn repertoire of *Play School* and Wiggles songs as the children danced, sang and shook percussion instruments. He was a great hit and they loved the novelty of his electric guitar at close quarters. But to close he played a song that only Jessie knew—'Shadow'. 'Where, oh where, oh where is . . .' he sang as Jessie leapt to her feet and cried, 'Sadow,' pointing to her own on the wall as the children looked on, perplexed. 'Where, oh where, oh where is . . .' he continued and Jessie charged to another wall crying, 'Sadow, sadow' until finally, 'Where can shadow . . .' 'Be!' boomed Jessie as she rubbed a third wall all over with both hands.

'Stuart had to turn his back to the tumultuous applause,' Fran said, 'to hide the tears in his eyes as Jessie joyously called, "Dada! Dada! Dada!"'

In July, two months after starting at Waterford, Jessie was also offered a place at Matilda Rose Early Intervention Centre. Moderate hearing loss was a prerequisite and many of the children suffered from other disabilities as well. Matilda Rose was a breath of fresh air. Alongside a curious mixture of fun and mayhem, intensive one-on-one therapy was the order of the day. Someone was always baking, so it smelled and felt like home. Indeed, better than home. Here everyone greeted you with open arms as if you were their long-lost best friend, and no-one was warmer, more compassionate or more positive than Maree Rennie, the Director.

'Do you know the story about this centre and Maree?' one of the Matilda Rose girls asked me one day. Maree had been working with the intellectually disabled daughter of a very wealthy family. Matilda could not speak or interact, but when Maree made a little progress with her, Matilda's parents asked her to start the centre. It would be named after their daughter and Maree's initial brief was to work intensively with Matilda. 'Don't touch it,' she was warned by colleagues, who felt Matilda was beyond hope.

When I first saw Matilda Rose at age eleven, she was giving a speech.

The colourful characters at Matilda Rose operated in organised chaos with a love and dedication beyond any I've ever seen. Maree refused to let the children's disabilities get in their way of doing what 'normal' children do. Excursions were arranged all over town only to find out on the day there was no car to get there. Christmas parties were announced and no-one was ever sure of the date, but somehow it all worked out. The children were taken to museums, to aquariums, to beaches, to the Botanical Gardens.

One time Stuart offered to help. They were going to see a visiting ocean liner at Circular Quay. Maree wanted the children to get a close look, so they planned to take a small boat out on the harbour to circle around the huge ship. The very idea would have reduced me to a blithering idiot but nothing fazed Maree. When they arrived at the boom gate of the restricted car park she shouted to the guard, 'All the children are disabled!', confident the guard would show compassion, sweep open the gates and let them in.

'So what?' he answered curtly.

Eventually, after parking half a mile away, with children charging in all directions while others were carried, pushed in wheelchairs or tottered unsteadily on walking frames, they realised the ocean liner had gone. But as luck would have it, another slightly smaller ship had just arrived to take its place and after rounding up the children Stuart found himself on a small boat bobbing on the harbour amidst a disturbed beehive of excitement. None of the children knew what was going on, but for Maree it was important for them to get out and experience life.

It was a day that left Maree flushed and blushed as she spied a great romance burgeoning between Jessie and autistic Peter. It was a day that left Stuart on his knees wondering what the hell had hit him.

In the world of disabilities life's truly unsung heroes abound. Fran is one and Maree is another. At over 60, Maree had the energy of a teenager. Small with brown, bowl-cut hair and a sturdy determination, it was nothing for her to throw Jessie around like a baby. Jessie was stubborn and easily distracted but Maree, relentless in her pursuit, was determined to push through and develop what she saw. When Jessie would throw a tantrum, Maree would throw herself on the floor alongside, grabbing Jessie's hands firmly, and break into 'Row, row, row your boat', pulling and pushing her back until Jessie fell in tumbles of laughter. Maree saw a deep intelligence within our daughter. Like Stuart, she felt adoption trauma was the major issue. If Stuart and Fran are optimists then Maree leaves them in the shade and so, between the three optimists, I began to have hope.

As well as Waterford and Matilda Rose, Jessie was also attending the Shepherd Centre. The Shepherd Centre has been a godsend to many deaf children. The staff concentrate on teaching them to speak, not to sign. Jessie had been going there for over six months and these hour-long sessions were a grind for all of us. With your hand over your mouth you say a word and wait for the child to repeat it. Getting Jessie to respond, let alone repeat, was like getting blood out of a stone.

After each session we were given homework. The drill was

to articulate your actions so the child related word to action. 'Where's the key?' I'd boom theatrically as we reached the back door. 'Here's the key. Turning, turning,' I'd continue, hand over mouth, staring at Jessie who was banging on the door wondering when she might get in. 'O-pen!' As soon as she gets one word, she'll never stop we'd been told, but you must wait for the child to respond before continuing the action. 'O-pen' I would say again peering meaningfully, wondering if I'd waited long enough the first time. 'O-pen.' 'At this rate,' I thought, 'we'll be stuck outside all night.'

'Door,' Jessie finally said, her eyes screaming, 'this is a pain in the arse, for god's sake let's go and watch *Shrek*.' As *Shrek* came on the TV, I smiled. According to Stuart, she could do all this stuff, she just didn't want to.

'And who can blame her,' he'd say. 'She might have a lot of problems but she's not stupid, just bloody pig-headed. And if I'm anything to go by there's nothing wrong with that,' he'd conclude proudly.

It wasn't long before the 'intervention' became a habit that dominated all our waking moments. Mealtimes had us both speaking with our hands over our mouths. And after Jessie was asleep I would say, 'Dada, get a bottle of shiraz.' Stuart would get a bottle of shiraz. 'Dada, o-p-e-n the bottle.' Stuart would open the bottle. 'Dada, pour the wine.' Stuart would pour the wine. 'Dada, well done. Well done. Dada?'

'Yes?'

'Drink the wine.'

Every evening, once Jessie was safely in bed, I crumpled on the couch exhausted. It was a tough time. Ongoing medical appointments continued unabated: eyes, teeth, sleep disorder, genetics, paediatrics and GPs—nothing was left to chance. But Jessie came to hate doctors and their needles and probing fingers with a passion, and consultations were often rushed as her bellowing unnerved these seasoned professionals. The genetic team took photos and said there was no hurry for blood tests when they saw her level of trauma as they were confident she was in the clear. The sleep specialist talked to Stuart without examining Jessie at all while I played with her by the toy box outside to shield her from distress.

Jessie was constantly sick with diarrhoea, vomiting or a cold. I had to take countless days off work to look after her. When she was well I was rushing to Waterford, then work, then The Shepherd Centre, then work, then Matilda Rose. Stuart jumped in when he could but my stress was rising. The idea of giving up my job was untenable. We needed the money and I also needed it for my sanity. It was the only time I felt I could rest.

And Jessie's improvements to be honest were small. She was also becoming more fractious, to the point I dreaded picking her up from school. I would drive round and round trying to get a spot as close to the entrance as possible. It was the only way to avoid a hysterical screaming fit up the road where she would throw herself to the ground. While I battled a desire to clump her over the head at times, my little girl saw only love. She couldn't help it, but my struggle to remain calm was taking a heavy toll.

To our great relief Jessie continued to make solid progress in an important direction. She was becoming more and more affectionate by the day. She didn't quite cling to us as some children might, but we were solidly her parents now and she was welcoming of our cuddles and kisses. Indeed, she needed them frequently as she was now constantly waking through the night.

Dr Tony Wood (pseudonym), Jessie's sleep specialist, had been seeing her for nearly six months. Initially he'd provided us with a range of techniques including nasal sprays and small doses of Melatonin. Eventually Catapres was used in conjunction with Melatonin in ever-increasing doses. Each scheme would work for a few days and then weeks would pass before we could get the next appointment to up the dose or try something else. As her distress grew we soothed her with touch in the wee hours.

But as the months rolled by my 'groundhog day' existence began to feel like a jail sentence—in fact jail seemed abundantly preferable: there I could at least get some sleep.

CHAPTER 14

ANOTHER RED THREAD
Sharon

'That must be very hard on you,' I said to the counsellor, probing her eyes. I had gone to see her at the urging of a friend. Counselling has never been my thing and I probably entered with a closed mind. However, when she confided she 'really' understood as she had an autistic son, I found myself doing the counselling whilst surreptitiously eyeing my watch. If the truth be known, there was nothing she could do for me anyway. All I wanted was for it to go away and for Jessie to be normal. To alleviate the despair I walked every morning and chanted to myself—a turbo-charged, power-walking lunatic.

Not long after Jessie's fourth birthday Stuart went away for a week to Germany. There were no therapy classes, no scheduled medical appointments and I was on vacation. It would be just me and Jessie together. I was looking forward to spending every day with my little girl. Outings were arranged with other mothers and I couldn't wait to slow down, give her my undivided attention—and relax.

The first outing was a bushwalk to a small beach. I'm a very small person and images of Jessie halfway along a dirt track refusing to budge filled me with horror. 'We'll help; you never know until you try,' the other mothers urged. On the walk Jessie amazed me: scrambling over rocks with other children was a hoot. But at the beach my heart broke into a thousand pieces. When all the children were young Jessie's difference wasn't apparent to them, let alone an issue. Now they could talk clearly; their social skills well developed. But Jessie didn't respond when spoken to and couldn't talk, and they didn't want anything to do with her. I could see she was upset when they turned away from her. The entire afternoon, while the other mothers laughed and made conversation, I wrestled internally with a fierce protective urge to rescue her and run. But there was nowhere to run. We both had to get used to this because 'this' was her future.

Another outing was to a park with a Batch 13 member and her daughter. My spirits sank when, after returning from the toilet unsuccessfully moments earlier, a wafting stench indicated that the chirping soul shouting, 'Bah!' on the swing had needed a big 'dump' all along. Cleaned and back once again from the toilet amid smiling 'no worries', Jessie immediately saturated her nappy till it hung like a bag in her trousers. What did it take to toilet train a child? How did any mother do it! Days, weeks, months: for over a year I tried, following her throughout the house, all the while keeping myself light so she didn't develop a complex. I loved her, I truly loved her—her sweetness and innocence and the way she squeaked, 'Bah!' in delight—but inside I screamed with primeval madness: 'I can't take it anymore!'

As I looked at my friend's three-year-old who was toilet

trained, wearing sunglasses and unscrewing a lid on a drinking bottle, I did something the other mothers with intellectually disabled children told me never to do: I compared. And I despaired.

When Stuart arrived home from Germany I wept in his arms with the same tears of utter hopelessness that attended my infertility treatment. 'I can't handle it,' I whispered. He cradled me close because we both knew I had to.

'What's your problem?' I started telling myself. Look at the tragic fate of Belinda Emmett, dead at 32. 'You don't have it that bad; get a grip. Be happy, be strong. Don't let this drown you.' So I took longer walks in the morning and read books by the Dalai Lama at night and doubtless started chanting in my sleep.

All this went out the window when my doctor took a routine blood pressure test and then took it again and yet again with rising, white-faced alarm. I'm a hypochondriac at the best of times but when he told me that no amount of stress in my life could cause a reading this high—'do not pass go, you must have an immediate ECG and ultrasound on your kidneys'—I knew my days were over. Stuart, who was in Melbourne, flew home immediately.

Unsure I would make it down the road and phoning everyone I could think of, I entered the pathology unit for the ECG babbling like a hyena. It took some while for the nurse to convince me that my heart had a normal reading. I knew then it was my kidneys but as it was a Friday afternoon I couldn't have the ultrasound until the following Monday.

Throughout the weekend I scoured the internet. Kidney disease is a silent killer and one of the symptoms—all of which I had—was frequent urination. With a bladder like a peanut I now realised I had been dying for several years. Suddenly everything was in perspective. Jessie's disability wasn't a problem. This was a PROBLEM!

When Monday came and I found out I wasn't dying, the next scare came through Stuart. The doctor told him his triglyceride reading was so high he should be dead. A few days later another test revealed he might live after all, but like me would be destined to a lifetime of tablets.

Then I got pins and needles and numbness in my hand: 'the first sign of stroke,' I thought. That subsided but was replaced by a nasty rash covering my face. Incredibly vain, I wrapped up in a scarf in public. Then I started balding overnight! Clumps of hair were coming out by the fistful. Even Magnus got in on the act. When I saw him lying in the bushes I knew my little friend of 12 years was very, very sick. But it's amazing what $4000 can do. Disc problem fixed, he was back to bounding down the road, albeit bumping into trees because overnight his eyesight had failed.

Desperately needing a break, I went away for the weekend with a girlfriend to relax. She talked me into seeing a clairvoyant, who talked about Jessie. 'Two awful bits of news about my daughter had turned my world upside down,' she said. She was right: the hearing impairment and global developmental delay had done just that. There was one more to come. It would knock us both to our knees but it wouldn't kill us. After that life would get better. I heard only the last bit and left her room a confirmed believer.

The end of year Christmas party at Matilda Rose was hilarious. Stuart offered to play guitar to keep all in tune. Parents packed the room and clapped ebulliently as the children were brought in. All had been assigned parts in the Nativity and Jessie was an angel. With her rosy lips, radiant face and black mane of hair against the white robe, she took my breath away. Like most of the children Jessie didn't know what was going on. They had been rehearsing since March. Soon the room was filled with carols as parents sang their hearts out watching their children walk off in different directions while others were spinning objects or falling off stools. Jessie became engaged in a twirling frenzy with the cord on her robe. When the concert finished to a massive ovation all the children, some now at the other end of the room, stopped to bathe in the applause. It was brilliant.

In the new year, both at school and Matilda Rose, there was growing excitement over Jessie's development. They could see a potential in her that intrigued them. As far as they were concerned the jury was out on the Tumbatin diagnosis; they saw a perplexing intelligence in her. A mother I met at Matilda Rose related how her hearing-impaired son had been given the same Tumbatin diagnosis. He was now developing as a normal eight-year-old boy. Even the paediatricians were divided about Jessie. In a follow-up letter to Tumbatin, our paediatrician, Dr Simon Brooks (pseudonym), wrote he saw no autistic tendencies in Jessie. I began to wonder if my optimistic husband had been right all along—that Jessie's slow development was that of a deep soul traumatised by a world that had hurt her.

Everyone's efforts began to bear fruit. Miraculously, toileting was solved by a $300 'Pants Alarm'. Here nodes are attached to the undies and connected to an alarm pinned to the child's back. When the child urinates the alarm goes off. Once it does, your high, shrill scream of 'Stop!' frightens the bejesus out of the child. Then you whisk her to the toilet to finish what had started, and once done she is showered with treats and praise.

The bathroom was stocked with sweets and Jessie, with her hearing aids and bionic pants, was a mass of wires. Within a fortnight she was toilet trained. It was a momentous turning point and life suddenly 'was trending upwards', to use the words of Magnus's vet.

By April we returned to Tumbatin full of pride. Fran, Maree and ourselves had seen massive changes and, according to one of the hospital social workers, Jessie was a completely different child. Tumbatin did not agree. They diagnosed autism as well as global developmental delay. This time it wasn't 'moderate', it was 'moderate/severe'. Funnily enough, we didn't bat an eyelid. I was now sure Jessie didn't fit into the box of their standard diagnoses.

'Stuart,' I screamed on the way back to the car. 'Remember the clairvoyant! The third thing will knock you to your knees but it won't kill you. After that things will get better!'

'What else did she say?' asked Stuart a bit too eagerly. It was alright for me to believe in such things, but he was supposed to be the sane one!

'She's got it!' cried Maree. For months she had been trying to get Jessie to draw and say the word 'circle'.

'Kirkle,' Jessie squeaked again, leaning over a page littered with ovular squiggles. 'Kirkle,' she squeaked all the way home, milking our praise for all it was worth. But there was a price to pay. In no time at all bold, black circles covered all our walls.

Soon after, Jessie completed an eight-piece puzzle and Maree was beside herself: 'You're not delayed,' she announced to my child, who was now destroying the entire puzzle and starting again in search of more praise. At The Shepherd Centre too Jessie was following directions, enunciating sounds and commanding a wide range of words with understanding and increased concentration.

'You have to go to the next session!' I shouted to Stuart over my mobile as Jessie and I walked back to the car from The Shepherd Centre. 'Jessie was amazing!'

Amazing her progress was. A year before she was blank, like a dead thing who didn't speak, let alone repeat words. Now she responded to her name and labelled up to a hundred words. She was much more active and could partly dress herself. She had stopped rocking and twirling. I could play simple picture games with her. She suddenly wanted to interact, particularly with boys. Boys didn't notice she couldn't talk, they were happy to chase her. There was another leap—water. After a year or so she'd developed an inexplicable phobia, but now she loved wading pools again. Here speech wasn't required and she got the interaction with other children she craved by splashing and being chased. She liked it so much that she often left a rather large seeping present in her Little Swimmers that saw me run for the hills while Stuart whisked her out before anyone noticed.

A year before, Jessie was scared of slides and viewed climbing ropes as alien objects. She now clambered up ropes to slides and sent herself hurtling down the other side. She also developed a love of batting and was brilliant at hitting a tennis ball. Rarely missing, she connected with tremendous vigour and broke several toy rackets before finding one that was hardy enough to withstand the slams. She loved that racket so much she took it everywhere—even to bed.

Life was looking up and I thought I might give the chanting a miss.

I can't stop myself from jumping out of time here to the end of the year. Jessie had been at Waterford eight months. When I arrived to pick her up she was on the floor with all the other children, listening and paying attention. Without any fuss she got up, went to the sink, got a plastic cup, poured herself tap water and carried it quietly back, resuming her seat. It may sound like nothing for a child who is nearly 4½, but for Jessie it was a gob-smacking transformation. Another time, the other special needs child, Dougie, who was deaf and also had cerebral palsy, was asked by Fran to get water for himself and Jessie. Dougie, whose intellect was fine but whose hands and body jerked cruelly, had a hard time holding anything. By the time he returned in his support suit and walking frame the water had flown everywhere. It was the stuff of comedy as Jessie tried to get the cup from Dougie, whose hand continually jerked in another direction. No-one stepped in to help. Fran believed in giving them respon-sibility. The look of triumph on their faces as they 'drained' their empty cups was one of the most emotionally uplifting experi-ences I've ever had. They were being treated just like 'everyone else', like equals.

After a three and a half year wait, on August 7 2007, Mei-Bi Yang, 2½, from Guangdong in southern China, came into our lives. Once again photos had been sent and this time it was more than I could bear.

This is what I wrote:

> Oh my God, they have sent the photos of Mei-Bi to me. I am almost too terrified to open them. I am here sitting and looking at the attachment. What if I don't like the photo, what about her age—that has to be a problem. I am so hoping she looks normal and alert. Oh my God! Well, Sharon—here we go.

What struck me immediately was how sad she looked. She was staring straight at me and as I leant into the computer and searched her eyes closely a warm glow permeated my body. This time it was a totally different experience. I printed the photos and took them to work, proudly showing them to everyone. All through the day I took her photos out and stared at them and by the end of the day the beginnings of a song danced in my mind:

In China they say that when a child is born
Invisible red threads connect to those the child is drawn
And no matter where you are, no matter where you be
These red threads are your destiny to me.

CHAPTER 15

LIKE LONG GRASS ON A GUSTY HEADLAND

Stuart

When I was young I bought a Frank Zappa album called *Weasels Ripped My Flesh*. On the cover was a man shaving his face with a weasel, holding it as one might an electric razor. The weasel's jaws were wide open and there was a wicked, ravenous glint in its eye. The flesh on the man's cheeks was jaggedly rent. The morning after we arrived in Guangzhou, following a nightmarish trip with Jessie, my face looked like I'd been shaving with Zappa's weasel. Alive with a crimson psoriatic rash, and with white chunks of flaky skin tumbling with every tiny movement, it was raw in many places and tender to the breath of a zephyr. I was also jumpy because I'd stopped smoking in yet another pact with my darling Sharon.

'Oh my God . . .' marvelled Sharon, taking in the White Swan's massive, open-plan hotel dining room, which hugged the Pearl River and stretched as far as the eye could see.

'Pan right,' I said, pointing to a spectacular internal waterfall that tumbled from a temple on high with the force of an inland river in the Kimberley during the Wet. Its noise prevented normal conversation and sprayed us as we moved down the passageway. We were travelling well above our normal price range but it was worth it.

This time we were in Batch 32, and luckily one of the couples had a six-year-old son adopted from Korea. Lachlan, whose boisterousness worried his parents, thrilled Jessie, who loved his chasing games. And Lachlan didn't give a toss that Jessie couldn't converse; instead they thoroughly enjoyed each other as he whizzed her in the stroller like a rally driver.

On the first morning, with Lachlan in tow, we ventured outside. The hotel grounds boasted massive palms several storeys high which shielded a giant, shimmering pool, and as it might have been for Alice in Wonderland we followed a winding path that led to a magical passageway of dense ferns and a vibrant explosion of red, lilac, pink and white trumpet-shaped blooms. On the other side, a vast complex of pools was fed by yet another waterfall. This second pool, sheltered from the hotel proper, became the ideal setting for Batch members in the days after the baby pick-up, providing a closeted world where we all drew our new children close.

If Jessie and Lachlan weren't running and screaming around this hideaway, they were splashing and squealing in the wading pool. As Jessie bashed Lachlan's father over the head with her cricket bat she bathed in his laughter—and Sharon bathed in hers.

When the big day arrived Sharon was all at sea with a mix of terror of the unknown and concern for Jessie. Jessie didn't understand she was about to get a sister, and Sharon was over-the-top attentive. Yes, Sharon was excited and anxious about the new arrival, but Jessie's welfare was also at stake. She sensed it would be a juggling act requiring great skill.

'Don't worry if the first poo takes a while to come,' Sylvia, our guide, counselled us on the bus. 'Don't worry, if the stomach is still soft, still soft, not hard, no problem,' she added. We all sat taut and stiff, frozen on the outside, flashing currents of nervous energy rippling on the inside.

'Today, today, today . . . we pick up the babies . . . we pick up the babies. Everybody out. Everybody out. Ninth floor, floor nine,' said Sylvia, who'd clearly been trained to repeat herself. In the foyer Sharon handed me the video camera and took Jessie's hand. It was my job to capture 'the moment' when Mei-Bi arrived.

So here we were, about to enter a Chinese baby shop once again. And it felt just like that. Reminiscent of a Myer Boxing Day sale, there was a crush of people spilling out of the elevators clutching brand-new babies. We were on a conveyor belt with hundreds of others that day. At some stage soon we would pass by someone with a spanner who would attach a baby with a little flourish and then send us on our way.

In the waiting room I was hopelessly nervous and struggled to keep my hand on the video camera steady. I kept checking whether the camera was on or off. 'Good, it's on,' I thought. I panned across the entire group and saw that all eyes were fixed on the door on the far side, unblinking. No-one's eyes left that connecting door for a second, their focus as intense as sprinters waiting for the sound of the gun.

Mei-Bi was the first one brought out. Suddenly she was just there standing in front of us, holding her carer's hand. Sharon at first reeled from the shock, it was all too quick, but then she was ecstatic. 'Look, Jessie Mei Mei, it's your little sister.' Too keen, too nervous, I filmed the entire show without pressing the record button. That's right, I missed it all and to this day I feel like a goose whenever I think on it.

'She's just so beautiful! I can't believe it!' said Sharon as she raised Mei-Bi into her lap, cuddling Jessie Mei Mei close. Although nearly three, Mei-Bi looked no bigger than Jessie Mei Mei had at 20 months. She had delicate, fine hair which had been cropped into a cute, boyish style, and though she looked totally stunned, she didn't shy away when Sharon cuddled her.

Sharon's excitement was boundless. 'Look, look. Look how beautiful she is. Jessie Mei Mei, it's your sister!' she effused as Jessie, bored with the hysteria, searched the room for Lachlan.

Away from our focus, our uninhibited rejoicing was replicated in every corner as each child was wheeled in. 'She's so beautiful!'; 'Look! She's eating already!'; 'Oh, so sweet!' Exuberant glee swirled through the room. It was the party of all parties and not a drop to drink.

Sitting on Sharon's lap, Mei-Bi was a rag doll of placidity, but there was a light tremor about her body and a dash of fear in her eyes, and when it was all too much her lips pouted. 'Ah, she's upset, it's okay, little one,' soothed Sharon, smiling broadly. 'Jessie! Jessie Mei Mei! It's your little sister!' she called again. 'Uh-oh, I think Jessie's done a little present in her pants, Stuart,' said Sharon placing Mei-Bi into my arms. 'Come on, little one, Mama's going to change your nappy.' With Sharon tending to Jessie I took Mei-Bi over to a couch and started playing with her tiny fingers, touching them gently one by one, but she never once looked my way, her gaze pointedly averted.

All the babies were out now and the atmosphere was

electric. Four batch members had babies just shy of 12 months, the others ranged from two to two and a half, to Mei Bi who was almost three. They all looked thin, pale, dazed, lifeless and oh so tiny for their age, but their new parents were aglow. The room rippled with congratulations and unadulterated joy and like a victorious Test Match crowd in a pub, everyone began to shout over each other. I thought how different this moment was to the rough and tumble of picking up Jessie in Nanning. None of these children had been fostered, they were all from orphanages and not one of them cried. Totally dazed, they were soothed in a swathe of human touch—and it was touch, we realised when we visited Mei-Bi's orphanage a few days later, that these children craved above all.

There was mayhem that day, but of a good kind. The cacophony of excited, noisy chatter was such you could barely think. It was like a crowded four-year-old's birthday party with proud parents rushing all over: 'Look, look, look . . . look what I got.' But in the midst of this swirling crescendo a young father in our batch stood stock-still, totally at peace, frozen in time. I'll never forget it. He looked down on his new daughter with the beatific gaze of the Madonna to the baby Jesus, just a hint of a smile on his lips, his eyes steady, warm and peaceful. His love was a blessing and his child understood. She looked back calmly, unflinching and unaffected by the rumble around. She was totally still too, totally at ease and gazing fixedly back into his soul. But suddenly I realised I had it wrong: the love in her eyes was the driver, the catalyst of it all. He was not blessing her, she was blessing him. Each remained oblivious to the rest, sustained in a moment of wonder as if they had finally found what they'd been searching for. At one point I could've sworn they were isolated in a warm, golden shaft of light: 'And no matter where you are, no matter where you be . . . these red theads are your destiny to me.'

In contrast it was clear Mei-Bi didn't feel her destiny was with me. Totally unresponsive and on the verge of tears, she wanted nothing to do with me. But once the four of us were safely cocooned in our room away from the raucous, excited throng, she leant into me for the first time and, as she sucked on the bottle I held to her lips, my heart swelled with joy.

Before the night was over Mei-Bi's name had morphed into her Chinese nickname, 'Bi Bi'. It was a term that Jessie latched on to immediately just as she'd recently warmed to being called Jessie Mei Mei. She loved the name Bi Bi and said it over and over. For her part, Bi Bi gravitated to Jessie, who was the only bit of this new world that looked familiar, her eyes following her wherever she went. But when we stood her up she just stared into space and rocked from one leg to the other like a chained elephant.

'Jessie Mei Mei, Mama's going to sleep with your little sister, okay?' Sharon explained carefully, holding her tight.

'Bi Bi, Bi Bi!' Jessie chuckled good humouredly.

'C'mon, Jessie Mei Mei, you're in with me,' I said, waving a sweet with a flourish. So Sharon slept with her new daughter from the outset, but she always put Jessie to sleep with stories and songs before relocating across the room. And sleep Jessie did. It was astonishing. She hadn't slept this well for years—right through the night until five or six in the morning! We couldn't believe it and were beside ourselves with relief.

It took a couple of days before Bi Bi, still rocking from one leg to the other, started to moan. It was the first sound we'd heard her make. 'Ah, that's good,' said Sharon, walking back into the bathroom, 'she needs to let it out.'

Bi Bi's crying didn't sound like a child crying. It was a guttural, whimpering moan; a mature-age, gurgling wail of anguish
that started in the depths and stayed there. Jessie's face scrunched
with pain. 'Bi Bi,' she called, her arm outstretched trying to reach
her sister. 'Bi Bi,' she called again plaintively. Then she wailed
along with Bi Bi, tears rolling down her cheeks, her face hor-
ribly contorted with the pain of it all. Jessie, who mostly lived in
a world of her own, oblivious to the discomfort of others, was
unaccountably stricken with grief. What was going on? Sleeping
well and now this!

'What's wrong with Jessie?' asked Sharon, coming back
into the room. With Sharon's reappearance Bi Bi immediately
became calm and Jessie followed suit.

'Bi Bi was moaning because you left the room, how sweet
is that?' I reported with poorly disguised envy. 'And Jessie Mei
Mei was frightened for her sister. It wasn't about her. That's not
sweet, that's a miracle.'

'She doesn't know how to cry, poor little thing,' cooed Sharon enveloping Bi Bi in her arms, colouring in her little face with
kisses.

'Bah! Bi Bi, bah!' blurted Jessie as happy as could be as Sharon drew her close as well.

So began Bi Bi's refusal to have anything to do with me.
Soon this became a running joke as the other dads picked her
up, no trouble, and delighted in bringing her over to me where
on cue she'd commence her little moans each time.

Within a few days Bi Bi was already becoming a handful: 'She's
thawing out much too much for my liking,' muttered Sharon,
trying to contain her as she bounced around like a little gibbon
on the bus and banged her window with a large pen that had

become her 'magic wand' weapon. Between times she kissed her mama all over when she wasn't munching on biscuits. Truth be known, Sharon was thrilled. Bi Bi's personality was flowering ever so quickly and it augured well.

But as I watched this action play out Sharon's mood abruptly changed. She looked across the aisle at Jessie sitting with Lachlan, full of concern. What was up? I couldn't figure it. The two new pals looked totally contented. In fact Jessie was euphoric. Sharon's brow was furrowed and her mind was racing. She peeled a banana, snapped it in two, and handed both pieces to Jessie, who passed one on to Lachlan. Two minutes later a handful of sweets was placed in Jessie's open hand and the two children gratefully shared the bounty. A packet of crisps soon followed— Sharon had scrunched up the contents so they would be broken into hundreds of tiny pieces. Jessie held the bag and once again the children happily shared, with Jessie doling out little handfuls to her grateful, wide-eyed friend. And so it continued. Indeed everything we had was doled out in a continuous stream. Still I had no idea what Sharon was doing.

Finally when Sharon produced two little poppers and handed them both to Jessie, and Jessie duly handed one to Lachlan, I got it. In the wading pool and when chasing each other in the luxuriant grounds of the hotel Jessie and Lachlan had got on like a house on fire. With Jessie in the stroller and Lachlan driving exuberantly down the pathways they were perfectly matched and Jessie had something to offer. But containing them in a bus for a six-hour round trip to Bi Bi's orphanage in Yangjiang was another story. 'Get away, get away, you're stupid!' the little girls had cried on excursions back in Australia. Sharon had immediately seen the danger and rushed to Jessie's aid to nip it in the bud. She engineered it so Jessie constantly had something to offer Lachlan—simple as that. Never once did she relax in her quest to shore up Jessie's new-found companionship and Jessie beamed for the entire journey. I'd never seen her look more beautiful.

Like an animal in the wild Sharon had sensed danger well before the rest of us and instinctively moved into overdrive. She saw Jessie, her child without language, with a friend for the first time and she did everything in her power to preserve their communion. Driven by profound love she scrambled and succeeded. That's my Sharon and that's why I love her.

'Warmly welcomes all the leaders, friends home and abroad come to see us' was emblazoned on the orphanage wall. In the courtyard several grime-encrusted urchins—older boys with disabilities—roamed aimlessly before being quickly herded away from us. One sunny character, about ten, escaped the net and came up to me, self-consciously touching a large, unsightly growth protruding from his temple. He had tropical ulcers all over his body. Did he have a disability? He certainly loped around like a wounded ape, but an unmistakable spark appeared to be trapped within; he seemed so bright and 'with it' and appeared self-conscious and sensitive. In fact he had the same gleam in his eyes I saw in Jessie's—an understanding condemned never to be expressed. Yet how cheerful he was. I took to calling him Dizzy because he liked to flop his head to one side and inflate his cheeks like a bullfrog, just like jazz trumpeter Dizzy Gillespie in full flight. But my heart ached in sorrow with the notion that this boy might have been anything had he not been a product of the orphanage. 'What if we'd never adopted Jessie? What would have been her fate?' I thought and shivered all over.

Jessie was delighted when she spied a children's playground, and she let her anger be known to the city of Yangjiang when I carried her up the stairs to an immaculate function room where the director was to give a speech. For Jessie it just wasn't fair, and the planned refreshments and address were quickly aborted as she cleared the room of all but us. Eventually she got her way and I took her down to the playground, with her hollering the whole way. Sharon cast a sympathetic eye but was busy quizzing the director, knowing this would be the only chance we would get to find out our child's history. 'Bi Bi is an extrovert,' he said, but three days earlier a carer had relayed she was a very quiet child.

'I don't think they even know who she is,' Sharon said later.

By any standards the playground with merry-go-round, spinning 'cage', slide and climbing apparatus was impressive. The boys we saw before, aged 5–12, were milling around again. Many had scars and lumps on their heads and half-crippled walks born of deformities. Most had obvious intellectual disabilities. Dizzy gravitated to me again. This 'elephant boy' adored having his photo taken and many times he moved his face right up to the lens, squashing his nose up against it as if he was trying to see what was inside, all the while waving his arms in a disjointed dance. At other times he made faces, pulling his mouth wide with his fingers or giving a reprise of his bullfrog act. Other times still, he was quiet, his grin downgraded to a wry smile, and again I sensed a keen intelligence floating beneath the surface.

Sharon's diary entry best describes what happened next:

Stuart took Jessie to the playground after her disruption. I left them there and followed Brigitte and Paul up some stairs. When the door opened the room was full of little children about one to three years in pink tops and orange shorts. They were everywhere; most desperate for kisses and hugs. The room had four rows of cots which were just iron-sided bare boards. They came climbing over each other to get to us and to get a hug. Bi Bi was with a carer doing her little moan, she feared we'd brought her back. I rushed over and held her to me. The carers were surprised, I think, that she was close to me after such a short time. She barely seemed to know them. They pushed her former playmates towards her but she didn't care nor seem to recognise them. She started pushing the children away and moaned to be picked up.

I didn't want to leave. There was one little girl who I was kissing and kissing, again and again. It was as if she'd never felt affection before in her life. I was kissing them constantly and holding as many as I could. Those little faces, devoid of love and touch, will remain with me forever.

Lachlan's dad came over to the playground and urged me to go upstairs with the others. He'd stay with Jessie and Lachlan. 'Come upstairs to see the healthy babies!' called our regional guide, Nicky, cheerily waving me over.

In Bi Bi's dormitory some of the children flocked around me while others stayed at the other end of the room, rooted to the spot. Almost all were rocking from one foot to the other, swaying rhythmically like long grass on a gusty headland. The room was spotless, white tiles on the floor and walls—toys nowhere to be seen. One toddler against the far wall lay on the ground, wide awake, staring at the ceiling. Another, terrified, hid in a dark enclave, refusing to leave the shadows.

While holding the camera, Sharon got down on her haunches to be closer to their level and was soon swamped with eight or so trying to clamber on her. The obvious trauma aside, these 'healthy ones' looked by and large reasonably cared for. I too got low to the ground and soon found a toddler in each arm. Then four more tumbled in. They pulled at my shirt sleeves and trouser legs to get as close as possible as they stared plaintively into my eyes. One was half choking me from behind as she frantically wrapped her arms around my throat. I got to my feet and kept picking them up and holding them tight, one after another, but when I put them down the inevitable rocking recommenced.

Sharon was overwhelmed as they crawled all over her. 'They're incredible, these little babies. I'd just like to take them all. It's not fair. There's lots of older ones here with no chance at all. Look at them, why can't we take more? They're just craving affection. It's broken my heart.' It broke *all* our hearts.

Sharon resembled the old woman in *Mary Poppins* feeding the birds as the children mobbed her. She fed them with cuddles and kisses. In the end, when she gave the children a book and squeaky toy, there was an avalanche of excitement. All the while, Bi Bi wouldn't let her mama go for a second.

'Did you go in and see the toddlers in Bi Bi's room?' I asked one of the dads who'd just returned from the 'baby' orphanage down the road as I rolled Jessie Mei Mei back and forth in her stroller. Shaking his head with a stricken look and tears brimming in his eyes, he recalled the terrible screams he'd heard coming from the upper building. These had so upset him he couldn't face it. He'd never forget those screams, and dabbing his eyes with a handkerchief he pointed to the window of the immaculate function room, shuddering.

I didn't know what to say; would the truth humiliate him? 'Oh, bugger it,' I thought, 'he'll find out anyway.'

'Mate, that was Jessie,' I whispered, trying not to laugh, slapping him on the back to show I thought no less of him.

We were both saved from this awkward moment when our

guide, Nicky, loudly called for us to jump on the bus to go. As the engine started, all four of us knelt on the seat looking out the back window, waving madly. 'Bye ... bye ... bye ...' Jessie called, whacking the glass with her plastic bat.

As I watched Dizzy through the back window I thought once again of what might have happened to Jessie if we hadn't adopted her. Her misfortune would have pushed her to the bottom of the pile in China and she would have suffered, of this there is no doubt. I'm not religious at all, especially not in any 'worship' sense, but at that moment my soul trembled with gratitude and I found myself thanking God for Her grace with all my heart.

ORPHANAGES IN CHINA

Stuart

Having now adopted two children from China we feel the need to break from our story and share, as a brief aside, what we've learnt about Chinese orphanages and China's international adoption industry. The plight of children in these orphanages will shock many. But we are not here to judge, just report what we've seen and heard first-hand. We are mindful that the massive scale of social issues in China is almost beyond our comprehension. We are also mindful that there is much in our incomparably affluent world that doesn't pass muster—a world where dogs are given vitamin supplements and fish are taken to the vet while hundreds of thousands of us are homeless or languish with disabilities effectively without support.

Of particular interest is the fact that in China, adoption allocations have dropped to a trickle in recent times. For prospective adoptive parents over 45 in Australia, China some years ago

152

became the only choice and the number of applicants swelled over time. In the early days, once your papers were sent to China, you'd be allocated a child just a few months later. At the time of writing, the prospective wait for new Australian applicants may be as much as ten years. How did this happen?

It's curious how the West transplants its own emotions and ethics as if they were universal on the rest of the world. Throughout the DoCS adoption seminars, much was made about the suffering of a Chinese mother forced to give up her child. This made sense and made us deeply sad. But feedback from some of the Chinese we have spoken to presents another picture.

'How do women feel when they are forced to abandon their children?' Sharon asked a family planning clinic worker in rural China through her daughter, who now lives in Australia:

> In cities now it is very different but in rural China where I work, life is very hard and people are very, very poor. Having a son to work on the farm is important for the family's survival. The women know they can have only one child. They accept it. For them, having a child and giving it up is similar to a woman in the West having an abortion. Some may mourn the child they never had but most don't think twice about it. In fact, many Chinese women know they must continue to give their girls away until they have a boy. This is how it is in China.

Let's put that fragment aside and move on to what we saw first-hand. Jessie's orphanage in Nanning, Guangxi, was largely hidden from us, but there were glimpses. We were allowed to see the spotless foyer, but denied access to the children. When we opened the wrong door we were bustled away but a moment was all we needed. Writhing babies were heaped in a lump on the floor, crawling over each other like maggots over meat, as we observed earlier. Others were climbing over their cots on the verge of serious tumbles. They were unattended. And, just as that door was slammed shut, to the horror of one of our Batch members, her new baby was plucked from her arms and briskly thrown across a harsh tiled room like a basketball in a training drill from carer to carer during our visit.

The orphanage then proudly paraded four children, aged about 16 months, who suffered from shocking cleft palate deformities. They would all soon be adopted by Americans, we heard. 'See what China does, we even look after our special needs children,' was the unspoken signal. But why couldn't we see the rest?

Subsequently when we visited Bi Bi's orphanage in Yangjiang, Guandong, we were surprised because we were allowed to move around and explore as much as we liked. The Chinese were proud of this orphanage; it was one of their showcases to the world. The grounds and immaculate gardens would have done any facility proud. But when we went into Bi Bi's former dormitory the devastation of no touch, no warmth and no love was there for all to see as 40 children rocked rhythmically through sensory deprivation. The room was barren apart from their cots marshalled in rows, side by side. There were no mattresses and no pillows. Feeding was done by clamping a bottle to the side of the cot and leaving the child to fend for herself. Bi Bi, who had known us for just two days but had lived there for nearly three years, cried with terror when we, different looking, speaking and smelling people, put her down. Throughout our visit she turned her back on the carers and grappled Sharon tightly.

This was just one orphanage and the sight of such deprivation will linger with us forever. Other Batch members got babies from an orphanage just down the road. All the babies had bald patches on their heads from lying on the hard bed boards of their cot all day. One child Sharon saw in a Sydney playground had a head completely flat at the back. She was around 16 months. Other adoptive families we've encountered brought back stories of children with rope burns on their wrists from having been tied down. Others actually saw children tied in a standing position to their cots.

Kay Bratt's deeply affecting *Silent Tears: A Journey of Hope in a Chinese Orphanage* provides another first-hand account of a 'standard' orphanage. In the book's 400-odd pages there is a death or major tragedy every 20 pages or so. The handful of carers can barely cope with the daily routine of feeding, bathing and nappy changes and often violently take their frustrations out on the children. In this hopelessly under-resourced world, for most of the day, there is little choice other than to leave the babies lying in their cots unattended. For the toddlers toys are banned because they can lead to disputes between children. On some occasions the children are simply seated in chairs against a wall for several hours to keep them manageable, and those who don't comply to the letter are ruthlessly beaten.

In the lead-up to the 2008 Beijing Olympics the Chinese started saying there were no girls available for adoption—the supply was running out. With higher standards of living, an increase in local adoption and better family planning, China was dealing with its problem, or so the message went. But when Sharon and I were in China to collect Bi Bi in late 2007, well after the so-called slowdown had commenced, we saw lots of little girls—toddlers—waiting to be adopted. Other Batch members told the same story when they went to orphanages in other parts of the province.

Tragically, China says around 70 per cent of orphans now are special needs. One of the reasons the 'special needs' category is so high is obvious—once a child turns three she is immediately reclassified as 'special needs'. Given the deprivation of the first three years there is some sense in this. But at Bi Bi's orphanage there were many children around her age—just a few months shy of three. There is no doubt the bulk of her companions would not be adopted in the little time remaining before this · reclassification took place, and once it took place, they would become indistinguishable from the limbless and the brain dead.

In other orphanages our group saw it was the same story— lots of older healthy girls and not a boy in sight. In light of this, the alleged shortage of children—and girls in particular—is surely propaganda. If this is right, the tragic consequence of the 'slowdown' of recent years is that countless innocent children will spend their lives in institutions never knowing the touch and love of a parent, when around the world there are thousands desperate to adopt them.

'Your child is a lucky one,' said another Chinese acquaintance of Sharon's, herself a mother:

> Those who are taken to orphanages get looked after but a lot of children are kidnapped, some are put on the streets to beg for others. Often they are disabled and their legs are broken or whatever so they get more money for these people. If you ever take your girls to China be very careful in parks as the Chinese wouldn't know these were the children of Western parents.

Kidnapping of women and female children is now rife in China. Little wonder, as there are 32 million more men than women of marriageable age, according to recent reports. Is this the reason that the slowdown has occurred? Are the Chinese now keeping their orphaned girls? If boys are prized in China, why is it that so many have been adopted recently internationally, particularly in Australia? What started as one or two boys 18 months ago has become more like four boys out of every six children allocated at the time of writing. It is perplexing when girls are the unwanted ones.

On the other hand, what will happen to a population filled with young testosterone-fuelled males who have no way of ever finding a wife?

Part Three

CHAPTER 16

THE DIAGNOSIS

Sharon

24 May 2007—4½ months before Bi Bi's arrival.

Stuart has a particular gait where his arms hang down with the palms of his hands facing behind. Here he was, right on time, loping up the path, his thick fair hair slightly greying—that arty dishevelled look I so loved. I poured him a wine thinking I'd drink it if he didn't.

'She's got it,' he said.

I knew immediately what he meant. All this time it had been nagging in the caverns of our minds like a black shadow.

Simon Brooks (pseudonym), our paediatrician, had just phoned him. 'It's not an aggressive type,' Simon had assured. 'Mild, that's why they hadn't easily picked it.'

'Say it again,' I said, my heart pounding. 'Exactly, what he said.'

*

We walked into Sydney Children's Hospital two days later. So familiar to us now: the wait at the desk, the play equipment, the routine medical checks. We asked them not to do the height and weight checks this time as they always made Jessie cry.

Directed to another waiting room, we found the quiet emptiness ominous. A pretty, fair-haired girl of around four was pushing beads around a wire frame in deep concentration while her mother watched on. 'What's wrong with her?' I wondered. The child looked normal. But so too did Jessie. I wanted to ask the child's mother; to share my fear. But I didn't. Instead I stared ahead waiting, holding Stuart's hand.

Jessie, who had taken so long to show an interest in other children, sat next to the little girl and, picking up some crayons, smiled shyly. My heart tugged. She so desperately wanted friends, but with words failing her, struggled. I'd often seen disappointment flood her face as she tried to initiate contact, only to see her 'playmate' turn away, bored or disturbed by her strange behaviour. Some children can be cruel. She isn't like other children and she knows it. This little girl was kind. She handed Jessie a crayon.

Jessie looked striking; her fluorescent green top and matching skirt luminescent against her brown, swarthy skin. Her hair was tied in pigtails, two black braids attempting to contain thick, unruly, wild black hair. She was losing her baby plumpness and I could see the young girl emerging. Her brown eyes, large and wide, looked up at me. She smiled with the innocent delight that always made my heart sing. To this day Jessie's smile is an incredible experience. She smiles to herself as if sharing some private experience that belongs only in her world; a coy delight, astonishingly beautiful in its secret innocence.

The clock ticked. I squeezed Stuart's hand until finally, 'Jessie Neal'.

The geneticist, Richard Hay (pseudonym), towered above me: a dark-haired, gangly man who looked like some awkward teenager standing with his mum. He had the face of a boy, but his uneasy smile was unnerving.

'This is our genetic counsellor,' said Richard, indicating the elderly woman who looked like his mum. My head was whirling: 'Counsellors are needed when the news is bad . . . it's standard procedure; don't jump to conclusions.' Taking Jessie's hand, I followed them in.

Jessie likes men and was immediately enamoured with Richard. Giving the Cheshire cat a run for his money, she beamed flirtatiously and handed Richard one of the bunch of crayons the counsellor had provided; then another and another.

Handing things to people had become Jessie's way of making contact. The more she liked a person, the more they would be laden with whatever she could find to put in their lap. Many a night, male friends of ours would be piled high with teddy bears, books and dolls, their heads barely visible. Today she'd forgotten her plastic cricket bat. It always makes me smile to see Jessie tucked up in bed with her cricket bat on the pillow beside her. She loves that bat and when she particularly likes someone she hits them over the head with it.

We all laughed as Richard's pile of crayons progressed to children's books. Jessie, delighted she'd made an impact on Richard, dazzled us all with a smile and then, with an almighty thump, whacked Richard over the head with a book.

'She has Sanfilippo Syndrome,' he said in response to our frozen faces. 'It's an extremely rare genetic condition; in fact I've only ever treated one other case. An enzyme is missing in the brain, so sugars don't break down and . . .' He went on as Jessie searched for more toys to hand him, smiling every time, searching again for something to give this lovely big, handsome man.

'So what does it mean?' I finally asked after hearing terms like 'mucopolysaccharide' and 'acetylglucosaminidase'.

Without drawing breath Richard replied: 'She'll probably die around the age of 12.'

They say that when a shark bites, the body produces chemicals to shield the pain—thus, like the shark victim who's felt a knock rather than his limb being ripped from his body, I stared, mute, trying to comprehend. I swallowed hard, fighting to control the watering in my eyes as a real physical pain stabbed and lodged in my heart.

My little girl, vulnerable, trusting and so unaware of her fate, was still smiling, oblivious of the fact that the room had gone silent and that she was the reason. My beautiful innocent angel, unaware of the horrific journey her life would take before her cruel, untimely, senseless end. She was dying. I could taste tears in my mouth but had no strength to wipe them away.

'There are three stages of Sanfilippo,' Richard said. 'The first stage is when a child starts to lag behind their peers. This is the stage Jessie is in. How long she will remain in this stage is anyone's guess. The second stage is called the 'plateau'. Once a child enters this stage they can no longer learn new skills and start to lose the skills they have gained. This stage is very, very hard on the parents because of behavioural issues and the child's inability to sleep. It lasts around four years, and then the child enters the final stage, where the decline is steep and most die within two years.'

Tears were rolling down my face, my lips quivering; chest heaving as I silently gulped for air. I looked straight ahead, avoiding Stuart's eyes, knowing I'd lose the small control I had if he touched me. Stuart had always made things better, had always fixed things. I relied so much on Stuart and I didn't dare to see his strength in shreds.

Richard was drawing a graph. I knew Stuart, dependable and controlled, would be taking this in, I could ask him the details later. Instead I heard only fragments: 'Most never get toileted ... 18 months left to learn ... plateau stage ... slow decline ... missing enzyme ... sugars don't break down ... build in the brain ... brain damage ... most difficult stage ... hyperactivity, chronic sleep disorder, behavioural difficulties ... hard for parents ... drugs ... builds tolerance ... little effect ... ear infections, teeth decay ... chewing body ... loss of skills, toileting, language ... epilepsy ... choking ... pneumonia ... dementia ... spasticity ... falling over ... wheelchair ... deaf ...'

'Who looks after them?' was all I could utter.

'You do,' he said, somewhat surprised.

'The next phase is the final one,' Richard continued. His matter-of-fact tone indicated we weren't the only ones who'd been told devastating news.

'This phase is usually quite quick, no more than a couple of years. She'll lose her mobility, but because she's in a wheelchair the condition is easier to manage.'

He said this bit like it was good news.

'She'll have difficulty swallowing. As the brain can't work out whether to breathe or swallow she will probably end up choking on her own saliva. There'll be increasing bouts of pneumonia and that's what will eventually kill her.' Pre-empting inevitable questions from Stuart, he proceeded: 'There's no treatment or cure in sight, but there's good progress in palliative care so she'll be well cared for.'

'Will she suffer?' I asked quietly.

'No, her brain won't know what's going on.'

I no longer had a desire to control my sobs. I was angry, a lioness's protection breaking free; I was angry, angry at the medical profession that would allow such things to happen to an innocent child. 'Because if you think for one moment I will sit back and watch my child suffer, you're wrong!' I didn't care what he thought, I didn't care about the counsellor shifting in her seat nor how I sounded. 'If you're one of those doctors who believe in keeping the child alive at any cost, you can forget it. Do you hear me? Don't you DARE think I will sit back and watch my baby suffer!'

I felt Stuart's hand on my arm and I heard him quietly crying. I felt boxed in; everywhere I turned no way out; suffocated by horrific, sickening images from which I couldn't escape. They expected me to watch on as my little girl lost everything, to slowly watch her die, ending up in a vegetative state where she wouldn't know whether to choke on or swallow her own saliva. It was beyond comprehension, beyond endurance, and this would happen over the next seven years.

It was like a horrible nightmare where you wake up screaming—only in this nightmare you don't wake up. I felt like I was drowning, trying to get to the surface for air but sinking further down into dark waters of despair.

I wiped my tears, trying to hide my distraught face from Jessie's wide, innocent eyes. She was standing looking at me unsure what was going on. My lips quivered as I touched her hair. I wanted to kill someone, I wanted to say: 'Do it now, take her away. Don't do this to her. I wouldn't do it to my dog. Let her go. It's bullshit, moral religious bullshit to keep someone alive. Of course she's going to suffer! What's the point of her life?' But I nestled my face into her hair, her distinct odour filling my nostrils—the fragrance that one day I would no longer be able to smell. How could I lose this child; the tiny ragamuffin urchin with cuts on her little frightened face who had been placed in my protective arms just a few years ago?

What a pitiful sight we must have made as we walked through the hospital corridors that day. Stuart's shoulders shaking with sobs and I, weeping openly: two broken people tenderly clasping the hand of a bright-eyed Chinese child, unable to contain their grief.

They say time heals the pain. But for us each day ahead for the next seven years was going to be as painful as the day before. We would have to watch our child degenerate into a wheelchair-bound vegetable, bit by bit.

I wonder how often people like us walk through the corridors of Sydney Children's Hospital; how often the staff see such a scene played out. No-one seemed to notice, but two people openly sobbing as we were was surely difficult to ignore. We probably became an evening story; an 'incident' seen at the hospital, something tragic, perhaps involving the little girl. For them we would be just a story.

As we made our way to the car, noticing people coming and going as usual, I thought of lines from the Robert Frost poem, 'Out Out': 'And they, since they / were not the one dead, turned to their affairs.' If you've ever lost someone close you know how surreal it is to see the world continue as normal when someone you have loved has gone forever. You will never be able to touch, see or speak with them again; a gigantic, painful hole in your world hardly noticed by the rest.

'Sweetie?' Jessie said hopefully to both of us, as she looked up at the ledge above our kitchen bench where she knew the rewards for going to the toilet were kept.

She loved chocolates, but being conscious of her teeth and weight, we avoided giving her too many. That afternoon she must have thought all her Christmases had come at once as Stuart, returning from the corner shop, placed a bag full of every chocolate she could imagine into her hands. As Jessie gorged that day on ice-cream and chocolate, we did the only thing we could—we drank.

Normally, more than a few glasses of wine for me deposits a thumping hangover the next morning, and for some reason, should I drink before 5 p.m., I get a headache almost immediately.

It was midday when we poured our first whisky. Having finally given up smoking several months before, we both attacked a packet of cigarettes. In self-destruction, we smoked and drank throughout the day and well into the evening, yet not once did I feel the effect. It took about a month, as I recall, before my tolerance broke. It was then I knew I was finally coming out of shock and had nothing to protect my raw emotions, and would have to, somehow, find a way to cope.

So we sat there in the afternoon sun, surrounded by greenery cruelly sprouting new growth, and drank; drank, smoked and cried for the hopelessness of it all. If Richard was right, we had seven years left and then Jessie would be gone. I would never be able to touch her, kiss her, comb her hair or stroke her face. She would be gone. I cried and cried. I cried that Richard had said not many children with Sanfilippo ever get toilet trained, yet our little Jessie had. Admittedly it had taken several arduous years of trying and 'bionic pants' to get there, but Jessie had done it. Jessie had managed to be completely toilet trained— and now she would lose it.

The years of trying to gain language would all be taken away;

the years of special-needs therapy would all be useless. She had 18 months at most to gain more skills and then any learning ability would stop.

The odds, he'd told us, of Jessie having this condition were around 1 in 250,000. How could it be *Jessie*?

I thought of a story from one of our Batch 13 members. After years of infertility she lost a baby born prematurely at five months. The little girl lived for three weeks before her parents faced the heart-wrenching anguish of when to switch her life support off. Weeping bitterly, the Batch 13 member had cried to a friend: 'Why me?' The response was gentle, simple and an attempt to create understanding: 'Why not you?' Yes, her friend was right: tragedy surrounds us and it has to happen to someone, but I was a long, long way from acceptance. If there was one godsend in all of this it was that Jessie would never know what was happening. Her intellectual disability made grasping the simplest of things difficult.

That night as Jessie watched TV I sat close, poring over her features, my heart wrenching in the knowledge that this beautiful healthy child before me would all too soon be in a wheelchair, her body mangled by an obscure genetic disorder, so rare that Australian geneticists have to consult with those in the UK for information. I wanted to savour her as she was now, before this cruel condition overtook and started to deform her body.

I looked at her shining clear brown eyes, eyes that changed shape depending on her mood; tonight they were large, wide and open as she delighted in Elmo's antics on *Sesame Street*. I gazed at her lips: 'Oh to have lips like that,' a friend had once said. They were full and wide, perfectly shaped. As she watched Elmo, enthralled, they parted slightly in that beguiling, shy, coy grin.

I consumed her face, the strands of black hair falling over her eyes; her nose, so distinct and unusual with its uniquely flared nostrils. Jessie was a chameleon. Sometimes she appeared hard and yet other times she was strikingly soft and alarmingly beautiful. I looked at her long fingers and remembered Stuart rejoicing when we first saw her baby photo that she had long fingers made for the piano. I remembered when we'd first heard the devastating news of her deafness that his hopes of her being a piano tuner were out the window. This had been an attempt at humour in a situation of great sadness. Sadness that our child, diagnosed with a hearing impairment, may face difficulties ahead.

I felt the tears spring once again in my tired red eyes: oh, if only that had been the extent of it. For Jessie's sake, I mustered all my strength and held the tears in.

Jessie looked at me eventually and banged me on the head, emitting her distinctively joyful 'Ouch!' and giggling copiously as I faked pain. It was too hard and I left the room choking.

Stuart was lost in jazz in the other room. So I went upstairs and lay in the darkness. No-one could fix this and somehow, somewhere along the way, I would have to learn to live with this pain.

I lay in that room for a very long time and Stuart stayed listening to his music. Neither one of us wanting to put Jessie to bed, wanting to make her do anything she didn't want to do— for now, for ever: whatever she wanted, she had to have.

So many emotions went through my mind as I lay stunned, in the darkness, digesting slowly the things Richard Hay had said. I could hear sounds outside the room: cars in the street, a dog bark, a voice cutting through the stillness from passers-by going on their merry way. I couldn't move. She was going to die.

The little baby I'd held so many nights crying after she'd awoken from coughing or the fright from some nightmare. The tiny child I had nursed through those colds; all those colds that now made sense. 'There's something wrong,' the pre-school director had told us. 'She gets far too many colds.' Jessie had never been without a cold, it seemed, until we finally got her tonsils out.

The geneticist shivered when we told him she'd recently had that operation: children with Sanfilippo can die from anaesthetic. I wondered if that would have been a better end than the one ahead of her. But losing her would have been unbearable.

And now we were going to lose her anyway. There was no hope. No scientific discovery to dream of. This was a certainty.

I thought about Fran, Jessie's pre-school teacher, and how much she loved Jessie. Fran who a year ago had asked us coyly if she could take Jessie out on the weekend because her family was intrigued to meet the little girl she always talked about. I heard her telling me only a month before, with tears in her eyes, how at the family dinner that night the only thing her six children talked about was Jessie.

I thought about Jessie's foster mother, who had loved her for the first 18 months of her life. The woman who had loved her so much she sent a desperate letter addressed to 'Neal Stuart, ABC, Australia' and how, incredibly, that letter had reached us. 'If she cries and is naughty, please be kind to her because she is a good little girl.' The love from this woman who'd fostered her had touched our hearts, but as we got to know this little child we understood because Jessie touched so many hearts.

We wrote back telling how well Jessie was going and how loved she was, but after receiving the news of Jessie's hearing impairment we never wrote again. The news was awful, so what was there to be gained?

In the darkness I thought about her real parents. I wondered if they'd had another child, the so sought-after male child. I wondered if that male child had inherited the same condition, and would the mother wonder if this was her curse for giving up her baby girl? I wanted to tell her she was not to blame, but most of all I wanted to share this horrendous pain with someone else who loved my baby as I did.

Of course in China the background of an adopted child could be anything. Jessie's mother could have been single, an encounter with the wrong genetic make-up resulting in Jessie. I would never know and they would never know. I would never know if her mother worried whether the child whom she abandoned was being cared for and I could never tell her there were worse fates than those she feared.

'And they, since they / were not the one dead, turned to their affairs.'

I am essentially a happy person who seeks laughter in all situations; that night I knew my very essence had changed forever.

CHAPTER 17

FALLING APART

Stuart

Sharon had been pushing the medical authorities vigorously to find out what was behind Jessie's problem. Apart from a mild to moderate hearing loss there were no clues. So she pushed and kept pushing and eventually got a terrible answer. On 24 May 2007 the Sanfilippo diagnosis knocked us down for the count.

As we died inside, we did our best to see that Jessie's routine—pre-school, therapy classes—continued normally. In between, we walked and walked—across the local beach headlands, around Darling Harbour and through the spindly coastal scrub to the old pillboxes and the vast ocean beyond at Malabar—rugged up against the winter chill, just trying to get through the days. We never strayed far from water, and high on the headlands, head-on we faced the salty sea breeze that stung our cheeks with tiny pinpricks of drizzle and cast our hair flying behind us. We stayed like this, stock-still, arm-in-arm, gazing at the tempestuous ocean for long periods wondering how we would get through the years ahead. How do you watch your baby die?

The shock was so great we were numb all over, our brains seized, and we were afraid. We were in a place neither of us had ever been before. But truth be known we had been in shock for years. To find out that our 'healthy' daughter, aged nearly two at adoption, had a significant intellectual disability had left us reeling. I'll try to put the pieces back in place.

After she'd been with us for a year or so, Jessie, who'd once been passive and gentle, had become confusingly fractious. Sharon's diary, 1 April 2005:

> What's going on with Jessie? She cried again in the car as soon as she woke up. These days she cries, no, shrieks, every time she wakes. Today I pushed the car to the limit, desperate to get home and out of the screeching fit. It isn't distress because she does it every time she wakes, not at other times. I'm going to ask the other mothers about it—it's weird.

Walking, for Jessie, had been a massive issue right from the start. To help her, we tried to walk her every night but we got nowhere. By the time she was five she still did everything she could to get out of walking more than a few metres. When we forced the issue there was uncontrolled exponential wailing and then, over time, she started dropping to the road with ear-piercing screams that went on and on for no apparent reason.

For two and a half years there had been sleep problems too. This, more than anything, was the real killer for all of us. By the beginning of 2007 it was more than just waking up an hour after bed; it was waking up again in the middle of the night, unable to get back to sleep at all, and screaming inconsolably.

We were confused and desperate. The grind even before we knew the Sanfilippo diagnosis had begun to feel like a life sentence. Living with Jessie's disability was like running a marathon but there was no finishing line. We became different people. The stress on both of us was obvious and people were beginning to keep their distance; not that we noticed or cared. But now we had a devastating answer to it all—and when Dr Richard Hay told us every skill Jessie had gained would be lost and her sleep and behaviour would all become 'much worse', it was as if Mike Tyson had landed his vicious right and then continued to punch well after the bell.

And somehow all of Jessie's problems escalated exponentially around this time—language, hyperactivity, pacing senselessly back and forward, shortened attention span and, the big one, sleeplessness—all tumbled into uncontrolled free-fall.

We needed a long-term respite plan, in particular some overnight respite, to face the terrible future ahead. Sharon looked for three months and drew a total blank. The situation was so desperate I took long service leave to find a solution.

'I know you'll get something organised, Baby Boy,' Sharon said with her eyes full of hope, 'because if anyone can, you can. You always fix it.' But after a few weeks of 'doesn't fit our criteria . . . $300 a day . . . sorry she has to be over seven . . . we can put you on a waiting list . . . check again at the end of next year', the bleak reality was inescapable—there was nothing on offer from DADHC (Department of Ageing, Disability and Home Care) and its related agencies.

Nevertheless I pushed on. I wanted to weep but couldn't. Between phone calls my hands trembled so much I had difficulty lighting cigarettes. Fate had us on the canvas, she was putting the boot in, but we were saved by the bell. Two months after the diagnosis, Bi Bi was allocated and we saw her photo for the first time.

At the time Sharon wanted to talk to DoCS about Jessie, but a counsellor friend and former DoCS staffer warned her unequivocally—*don't!* To this day I thank God we never went down that road. When I look now at Bi Bi's joy in our loving arms, and reflect that at just short of three she was only weeks away from a life too bleak to imagine, it chills my soul.

Amidst our despair, adopting Bi Bi gave us something to look forward to, and new energy and the odd laugh now tempered the sadness. We had tried to protect Jessie from our sadness, but even with her brain falling apart she knew. Now that Bi Bi was on the horizon she seemed to pick up on the new spirit and was having fun again. She even regained some words and abilities. Her smile returned, she danced and clapped to music and once again identified some colours correctly.

'Our house has been silent for too long,' proclaimed Sharon, looking at Jessie. Jessie had loved adult parties so we threw one just before we all went back to China. We invited all the people Jessie loved. We had to keep our home as Jessie had known it: full of people, full of laughter and full of music.

Thank God for Bi Bi.

When we returned from China Bi Bi fitted in as if she'd lived with us all her life. She was effusive and loving right from the early days and always happy. If there'd been any concerns over difficulties from living in an orphanage for the crucial first three years of life they were soon swept away. Bi Bi was equally attached to both of us, lively and inquisitive and easy-going with Jessie. So with Bi Bi adjusting so well I was able to focus on our ongoing search for respite.

Jessie's sleepless nights had returned with a vengeance and we were losing our minds. Two or three hours sleep a night was the norm. The rest of the time she wandered or ran through the house unless you pinned her down. And along with the sleeplessness, and maybe because of it, behavioural problems tumbled in.

Jessie was fractious all the time. Well, looking back that's how it feels. But she wasn't. Often we had as many as two or three pretty good days in a row where she was sweet, loving and calm. Increasingly, however, every bit of her daily routine became a battle. Some days you couldn't feed her, dress her, do her hair or clean her teeth without World War III breaking out. You couldn't reason with her, you couldn't communicate; she just threw herself down and screamed.

Going out, even just to the park, was a brave act—there was inevitably a distressed scene which meant we were back in the car in minutes. Indeed the only thing that worked was driving the car aimlessly through the suburbs. This we did for many hours every week. It calmed Jessie better than any drug and seemed to have an immediate effect. Finally two places gave us hope.

The first was Bear Cottage, a hospice for children, which could offer a couple of days every three months or so. For Jessie's first visit it was arranged that she stay in a private room upstairs while Sharon, Bi Bi and I moved into a comfortable apartment downstairs and visited her during the day.

'It's lovely,' I muttered, straining to smile and show how grateful we were that they would look after Jessie. But it tore my guts out just to be there and it took every ounce of courage I had to keep my composure. We were given a grand tour past mountains of toys, TVs, a massive spa, games rooms—even a huge glassed-in, outdoor cubby house peacefully brushed by foliage, the 'quiet room'. Bear Cottage is a wonderful place for children.

When our guide said 'and this is the dining room; we have our own cook so all meals will be cooked for you,' Sharon began to cry because even though we tried to ignore it, we knew Bear Cottage—this large modern building set among sprawling, manicured grounds, and clusters of trees on top of a hill by the seaside at Manly—was a place where only dying children come to stay.

But we had something and after countless knockbacks we were deeply grateful. With renewed optimism I met the intake board at Allowah Presbyterian Children's Hospital, our second source of hope, later that week. Allowah, situated in Sydney's north-west, cares for children and young people with significant physical and intellectual disabilities. It effectively works as a long-term respite centre for many families rather than as a traditional hospital, though it is that too. At my first meeting a couple of months earlier it had been established that Jessie met all the criteria and I'd only seen smiles and encouragement.

'How did it go, Baby Boy?' Sharon shouted excitedly, coming home from work after my meeting.

'She's too mobile,' I said, averting my eyes. '*Apparently* she'd be straight in if she was in a wheelchair.'

'But they said they would take her.'

'Yeah, but *they* weren't the boss . . . even this mob can't cope,' I said bitterly, pushing a letter from Bear Cottage towards her that had just arrived. In it they lamented that during Jessie's visit the previous weekend she'd gone missing during the night, and had eventually been found having a joy-ride in the lift; an event which shook up the staff considerably. She could come again but they needed advance notice and lots of it. It was a resource issue; they'd need to get extra staff in.

Bear Cottage could still offer respite a couple of times a year, but Allowah, our main hope, was gone.

With all our options exhausted Sharon, at her wit's end, made a crisis call to DADHC. She was forced to leave a message. The crisis was genuine but no-one returned her call until embarrassed into it by another agency days later. 'Don't you understand there's nothing we can do!' the DADHC case worker said to me sternly after Sharon passed me the phone, too overcome to continue. 'I can report you to DoCS. Do you want me to do that?'

'If that's what it takes to get any help. We're drowning.' I said.

Sharon's diary, 20 November 2007:

The prospect of the day ahead tugs as the clock ticks by in seconds. How can I bear this? I put her favourite Chinese DVD on and hoped for the best but her screams have begun to wear me down. Her nappy was soaking but she flailed and screamed as I tried to get it off. It is a battle to get her dressed. I tried to hold her head but she roughly brushed off my attempts to clean her teeth . . . she won't have her hair combed and broke into screams, pushing my hand away, flailing again as she charged towards the door. The clock ticks. I am tired and drowning, choking gulps of air. I don't know how I can keep doing this but I know I have to. It's like being caged in a dark box knowing you can never get out. Why doesn't someone help us? Tears roll down my face—each day the same; the same inevitable demands from a mind out of touch, a mind that doesn't know she is killing the person she loves. Every day I chide myself for the negative thoughts that flood me—wishing she was gone. Every day . . . every week . . . months; when will it all catch up with me? Will my own sickness be punishment for my thoughts?

Lately I break down at the sight of joyous smiles between a child and parent, or from a stranger's sorry stare, or an innocent comment from an acquaintance who doesn't know—'how happy you must be finally having children at long last!' I want to scream: no-one knows what it's like. Years and years to go: she was normal, nearly two for God's sake—how did this ever happen?

She took my hand just now—calm—and put it around her body. 'Keep me safe, Mummy,' she might've said if she could speak but inside me a voice screamed: 'Please, just go away!' Her shining eyes; her hair half in, half out—her thick unruly wild hair: my wild child. Oh how I love you.

One night in late November it was my shift with Jessie. After ninety minutes of lullabies I got her to sleep.

'Something'll come up, Baby Boy,' Sharon said when I finally emerged from the bedroom. There was peace at last and we just sat there soaking it in.

'Time for bed,' I said. It was 11.30 p.m.

'A-schoo, a-schoo!' Jessie squeaked as she appeared on the porch holding her cricket bat, Sharon's akubra perched precariously to the side of her head. I stood up wearily but Sharon pushed me back down.

Through the window I saw Jessie jumping on the couch like it was a trampoline, pointing at the TV and rubbing her hands in anticipation. 'Back to bed little one,' I heard Sharon say as Jessie plaintively changed tack: 'Melmo?' then 'Sadow?' she squeaked hopefully, bouncing up and down on her bottom and crossing her little legs as she stared at the blank TV with bright shining eyes.

She looked so beautiful when she was happy. 'Christ,' I thought, 'all she wants is to watch *Play School* or *Bear in the Big Blue House* and then she will die.'

'A-schoo—bear!' she squeaked, pointing desperately for Sharon to understand, lips puckering as she turned her cricket bat nervously.

'Don't!' Sharon said when she returned to the porch, knowing she'd done the wrong thing. I smiled at her tenderly, drained my glass, kissed her on the cheek and we walked into the lounge room together to watch *Play School* with the little girl we loved.

But it's reckless to break the routine. After finally going to sleep at 1 a.m., Jessie woke at 3 a.m. ready for a party, but when morning came all she wanted to do was sleep. 'What's going on?' said Sharon, walking down the stairs to Jessie's bedroom.

'I'm trying to get Jessie ready, what do you reckon?' I snapped.

'Don't get angry with *me*,' Sharon snapped back, voice strained.

'She wants to sleep.'

'She can't,' said Sharon, coming to assist as Jessie, hollering, wrestled me off and again tried to lie down.

'You tell *her* that!' I said pulling her up from her bed, wincing from the shriek in my ears.

'Don't blame me.'

'I'm not, it's you going me,' I snarled.

'Oh piss off!' Sharon shouted over the din.

'YOU piss off!' I snapped as Bi Bi came down the stairs and started to cry.

'Now look what you've done!' said Sharon gathering Bi Bi into her arms. Smiling through angry brimming tears she started to laugh.

'Mummy and Daddy playing ... oh I love Daddy, love Daddy,' she said putting her arm around me. Quick to protect as much as Sharon, I hugged them both and we all began to laugh, including Jessie, who now seemed recharged and ready to rock.

But Sharon knew Jessie would be too tired for day care—they'd let her sleep all day and that would be disastrous—and there was no way I'd be able to keep going like this. She dialled work and looked at me desperately. 'Stuart, what are we going to do? We haven't slept in the same bed together for nearly a year.'

One of us always slept with Jessie so the other could get sleep and the rest of the time we cared for her needs.

'I don't know, I'll keep trying,' I said wearily.

'But you *have* been trying—for six months, and in a few more you'll be back at work,' she said, unable to control the edge in her voice.

'You do it if you think you can do better!' I shot back, tired and bitter at the lack of understanding and appreciation. My anger infused hers and unable to stop it, we snapped into an almighty screaming fit that the entire neighbourhood would have heard.

'*You* stay at home and see what it's like!' Sharon roared at the top of her lungs, not caring who heard.

'I *have* been at home!' I yelled, my face burning.

'But you know it's not *forever, you can escape!*'

'Okay, I'll give up my job, how's that?' I screeched, walking into the kitchen away from our wide-eyed children who'd never seen a cross word between us before.

'We both know you can't give up your job,' screamed Sharon, following. 'Meanwhile I have to hold down a job, cope with disrupted sleep, shuffle my work hours for medical appointments, cope with the fractiousness and take time off when she's sick *and* she's getting bigger but what the hell's new, hey? You'll be back to work but don't let it concern you.'

She knew how unfair that was. Wherever possible I took time off work to help—with everything. I'd taken long service leave, done everything I could. Frustrated, my fury knew no bounds. I slowly leant towards her and in a low, menacing whisper hit below the belt.

'You might not have had to take a day off if *you* hadn't kept her up when she should have been in bed!'

Tears bristled in Sharon's eyes. I had twisted her act of love, turned it into a weapon, and she stared at me with incomprehension. What had happened to us? We were teetering on a precipice of blame and resentment and one more false move would blow us to smithereens. Our once perfect love had lost all intimacy. We were in trouble, we both knew it. The anger in Sharon's eyes took on a hardness I'd never seen anywhere, anytime.

'You supercilious bastard,' she hissed. 'You think six months of home with me here most of the time to help is what it's like. You're so pious it's sickening.'

'Fuck you!' I screamed, knowing a line we'd never wanted to cross had been crossed.

'Fuck *you*!' she roared.

'I'm leaving!'

'FUCK OFF THEN!'

Raging at the injustice of it all I reached into the kitchen cupboard and smashed one condiment bottle after another on the floor and kept smashing them until the cupboard was empty.

As we stared at each other heaving, Sharon began to cry and cry and cry and for the first time I just didn't care. I was beyond comforting her.

The morning before our screaming match, Gerry, a close friend who'd stayed over the previous weekend, had felt compelled to write:

November 26, 2007

I'm so upset—need to write, need to write! I KNEW it was hard with Jessie but I NEVER realised how hard. Oh Sharon, you were always the most charismatic and beautiful one and you looked SO HAGGARD and my darling Stu, the quiet observing and thoughtful one, you were like the 'Cat

On A Hot Tin Roof'. I have never seen you smoke so much, jumpy and couldn't sit still. Little Jessie, my beautiful little Jessie, you've disintegrated—all the time, wandering from one end of the house to the other, handing you things, walking away, coming back, giving it to you, taking it back, giving it back . . . AND THAT IS IT—her entire communication—and it seemingly has no end.

You both love her so much, handing the toys back, taking them again, putting yourselves at Jessie's communication level but your eyes are full of DESPAIR and PAIN and AGONY . . . I HAD NO IDEA. Everyone's nerves are on end in that once beautiful, easy, fun loving home.

Then Jessie, at night, charging from one end of the house to the other . . . poor Stu. I wanted to go downstairs and help him but I was too tired after just one afternoon with Jessie . . . and the SCREAMING, that terrible screaming. I saw it once in the car way back, way back but that's part of everything they say . . .

And how much weight you've both lost!!!

I've never seen you together like that: Stuart, you couldn't look at Sharon and Sharon, you couldn't look at Stuart . . . for over TWO HOURS the most loving couple I know couldn't look at each other and then Sharon, you went into the kitchen to make tea and offered one to Stu . . . he came and joined you and you held each other and cried like your hearts were breaking . . . with all of my heart I LOVE JESSIE . . . BUT YOU CANNOT DO THIS TO YOURSELVES. No-one should have TO DO THIS!

In early December 2007 Jessie was admitted to hospital for a sleep study. Dr Wood, realising the gravity of our situation, had said, 'As much to give you both a break as anything'. As the nurses settled Jessie in I lay on the hospital bed, too exhausted to get up. When the hospital social worker, Heidi Taylor, turned up with some forms, she sat down beside me. As she probed

compassionately, I wearily recounted the brick wall we'd hit trying to get help.

'I'll call all the agencies in for a summit meeting,' she said.
'I'm a fan of summit meetings. I know the run-around families
get. This way they will all be accountable.'

At the meeting it was quickly apparent there was nothing on
offer except one-off, sparsely scattered 'emergency' respite. The
woman from DADHC had nothing to meet our needs. We knew
that already: she was the one who had reported us to DoCS.
Ironically, although all children with disabilities fall within
DADHC's ambit, their own rules and regulations prevent access
to ongoing out-of-home care for any child under 12. 'You have
no choice,' said the hospital DoCS liaison officer. 'You have to
relinquish her to DoCS, you can't go on,' she said gently, trying
to make us understand.

Sharon, who had been silently weeping throughout the
meeting, now cried openly at the hopelessness of it all. We
both knew the woman was right. We had a choice, but it was a
Sophie's choice. How could we live without Jessie—how could
we live *with* her?

To give DoCS a legal basis to get involved, we had to refuse
to take Jessie home from the hospital. At law, we had to 'abandon' the baby we loved.

When we finally agreed, many cried and called us 'brave'. (For
months afterwards we wrestled with what they meant. How
could anyone refer to our actions as 'brave'?)

The hospital phoned DoCS, and DoCS became responsi-
ble for our daughter's care under a six-month temporary care
agreement. This, we were told, was the only way we would get
out-of-home respite.

While DoCS looked for a place to put Jessie, she stayed in hospital waiting for the paperwork to be sorted and a house to become available. We visited her every day, aching to take her home, but unable to go back to how it had been. All we wanted, we told DoCS, was assistance in looking after Jessie, some respite from the pressure that was killing us. We weren't abandoning her, we wanted—needed—to remain involved. But it didn't work that way: when they found a place for Jessie it was in Newcastle, over two hours away.

DoCS like to keep the parents close to their children, a friend who worked for them assured us. We'd imagined some boarding-school model would come into play, but the brutal reality of Jessie's placement in Newcastle hit us like a ten-ton truck. How could it be their only option? How could it be that in a city of over four million people there was nothing at all?

To DoCS, our situation mattered not. Jessie was placed. Another crisis 'solved'.

CHAPTER 18

IN THE BEST INTERESTS OF THE CHILD

Stuart

Jessie's stay at the Sydney Children's Hospital at Randwick stretched for just over two weeks in the end. She was finally discharged 19 December. Rather than allowing her to be whisked away to Newcastle in the care of strangers we insisted on taking her home for the first few days and taking her up ourselves the following weekend. This surprised everyone. No matter what we said it never seemed to sink in that we'd 'abandoned' Jessie because we couldn't look after her every day without help. In short, we'd hit the wall but we weren't walking away. Indeed a curious development the day after Jessie left hospital showed that ongoing involvement from parents was something the system just didn't expect.

It happened like this. The temporary care agreement we signed with DoCS was designed to last for six months and when it expired, if we were still unable to have Jessie at home, court orders would follow. If during the life of the agreement we decided to take Jessie back—on the other hand—everything lapsed and that would be the end of it. But in DoCS speak *any* overnight stay constituted 'taking the child back'. They rang us up in a panic when they realised this. 'After you take Jessie to Newcastle,' they said, 'you'll have to sign a new agreement'. But it didn't stop there. As she was going to visit us three weekends a month we'd have to sign a new agreement after every visit. 'Perhaps you could both come into our office every Monday,' they suggested helpfully. We invested in a fax machine instead— another suggestion of theirs—which we used twice before someone higher up agreed that the written agreement could be amended by hand. Our 'as-new' fax machine collects dust in the attic to this day.

I smile at this now but no one was smiling then. Those weeks in December 2007 were fraught and tough. I've blocked most of it out. I can't tell you about my feelings, I simply can't remember. I won't allow myself to remember, not in any detail anyway. But I do remember that as Jessie's three-day sleep study drifted into its second week, the doctors grabbed the opportunity to experiment with her medication by intro- ducing speed and risperidone, a controversial anti-psychotic which had been prescribed to help with fractious behaviour and sleeplessness.

I also remember catching Sharon sitting by Jessie's bed at home, an empty suitcase open on the floor. She sat in the dark but as my eyes adjusted I gradually made out her face which was contorted in a grotesque spasm of grief. She was packing Jessie's clothes; stroking each item then placing it gently in a suitcase while tears tumbled down. At this very moment her little girl languished in hospital alone, in the dark, bewildered and frightened. Sharon needed to punish herself by packing Jessie's bags. 'She's all alone in that hospital and I put her there,' she whimpered.

'Let me do it,' I whispered, my voice trembling and broken.

'No, I'm a spineless traitor,' sobbed Sharon. 'I'm weak, I can't keep going,' she said angrily, slapping the carpet. 'I have to pack her bags. I want to hurt myself, I want to feel the pain,' she said gulping for air.

'Mama!' It was Bi Bi in the doorway. Instantly Sharon's unsightly redness from hours of weeping was replaced by rosy-cheeked good cheer and the broadest of smiles. The transformation was miraculous. Sharon skipped across the room and flicked on the light. I swept Bi Bi up and spun her around until I was too dizzy to continue. At the same time Sharon clapped a strict rhythm and sang a simple children's song in Mandarin about harvesting carrots.

I can remember too Sharon's anguished cry later that night when a heartless sniper struck. Kathy had been very special for Sharon, the two of them went back a long way. It's hard to imagine two people closer, or so it seemed. But Kathy's bullet, although not fatal, lodged in Sharon's body and will stay with her till the day she dies. To paraphrase her email:

17 December 2007

. . . why is it the case that an Australian couple can adopt a little girl from China and then abandon her when things get rough?

So I'm doing the only thing I can do and that is walk away. I don't want to see you again. I never thought you would take advantage of your little adopted girl to make yourself look important and then just abandon her. It's disgusting.

Lots of people have been calling me to express their anger.

I can make 'no excuses for you whatsoever'. People are urging me to put in a complaint to DoCS to make sure everyone knows 'Jessie was nowhere near as bad as you painted her' and it was you looking for an easy escape.

'You couldn't be bothered' to do the hard work. I look forward to seeing you everywhere in the media 'campaigning for all these children you . . . suddenly . . . care for'. But I bet nothing will change.

Is this why they called us brave? Was Kathy the voice of mainstream public opinion? At the very least she was probably reflecting the views of the shock-jock polemic where outrage is a constant bedfellow. Most of my life I'd watched dispassionately as these media manipulators dramatically picked their targets, relying on the ignorance of their acolytes and the entrenchment of ideas by the self-interested and the powerful—from tycoons to prime ministers—to win the day. Were we now in their sights? Of course not, it was just Kathy after all. But while I knew Kathy's views were of no consequence it was still an almighty kick in the teeth.

I thought I would never see Sharon at a lower point but I was wrong. In what follows I have picked out fragments of our dealings with DoCS in an attempt to understand why the next six months became such a paralysing and frightening experience—one that also gave us a shocking insight into how children can die under their care.

Yes, we could have taken Jessie back at any time but crippled with anguish, we couldn't. We simply weren't equipped to cope with Jessie's high needs, and a taste of respite had showed us how tortured our life had been. We are ashamed to say that returning to that was more than we could bear.

*

190

DoCS had a lot on their plate when we relinquished custody of Jessie. Over 300 new children had come into their care running into Christmas, and Jessie was just one more. They had placed Jessie with Allambi—a 'crisis' residential organisation which presided over hundreds of children spread through numerous houses in the Hunter region. It was 160 kilometres from home and we were forced to settle for a very formal three weekends' contact a month.

But DoCS also appeared kind and understanding. They would do their utmost, they promised, to find a more appropriate placement as soon as possible. 'Okay,' I thought. 'A temporary, crisis placement.' Temporary crisis. One-on-one care around the clock. We could probably live with that for a while. And, as my mother, Rae, and sister, Penny, fortuitously lived in Newcastle, we could stay with them over Christmas and see Jessie regularly during her first week away from home. It might work out in the end.

Just before Christmas we drove Jessie to her Allambi house and stayed a few hours to help her settle in with her new carer. Jessie was hopelessly dopey on risperidone and the Allambi staff was very attentive. She'd been on the drug for over two weeks and as each day passed she seemed less capable than the previous. 'It takes a week or two to settle down,' the experts had said. 'She'll develop a tolerance.'

But on Christmas Day at Penny's house Jessie shrieked all day long and bounced off the walls—a mad girl, her brain scrambled as she mindlessly scattered slices of bread around the house and hollered at shadows. Traumatised, the family retreated in the end to the numbness of television and sat in silence, immobile, unable to deal with Jessie's fractious frenzy. No one could believe the sudden change in her. When we took her back to Allambi we urged them to watch her closely and keep us informed.

By the time New Year's Eve came around we were back in Sydney and Jessie was making her first official visit. Maree, from Matilda Rose, had given us all tickets to the The Lord Mayor's party for disabled children in the Botanical Gardens. Jessie had always loved fireworks and the Lord Mayor's party on New Year's Eve was like having our own private box down near the Opera House.

As we approached the party mid-afternoon we took home video of giants on stilts, jugglers and clowns, and Rumplestilt-skin and a whole host of fairytale creatures jumping out from behind Moreton Bay Figs. Bi Bi had never seen anything like it and excitedly raced all over, fearlessly exploring every corner of the park—laughing and laughing. Her eyes sparkled, and her antennae were thirsty for each new happening.

Jessie was slumped in her stroller resembling a 90-year-old stroke victim, her head flopped to one side. When we spread out the picnic blanket she was dribbling from her mouth, shaking and falling over. She no longer knew who we were. She had been irritable and crazy on Christmas Day but now she was worse, much worse. Back in the stroller time and again she battled to get out, failed, and slumped back exhausted. Sitting on the blanket she fared no better. Her arms trembled under the strain of keeping herself upright only to collapse altogether in some sort of closed-circuit, *Groundhog-Day* nightmare. When I got her on her feet she staggered and fell. Her muscles had shut down. Handfed eating or drinking was impossible. Jessie was crumbling before our eyes. Rather than developing a tolerance to risperidone, there had been a cumulative effect.

As it started to get dark we moved en masse to the water's

edge to take in the fireworks. The children lit the way with an array of luminescent tubes that came in all shapes and sizes. Bi Bi was enthralled by this new magic and somehow managed to collect more than her fair share of these wondrous pink, blue and green light sticks. When the fireworks began I held Jessie tight and watched her closely. Safely in the dark a tear came. All the other children were in awe of the miraculous exploding light dance in the dark heavens above. Jessie's eyes were dead, totally dead and dark; just inert mirrors reflecting the dazzle over the water as she slumped downwards. In the end she insisted on facing the other way.

We had known something was terribly wrong during Jessie's first few days in Newcastle. Indeed she seemed so dopey it was impossible to tell what the impact of her move had been. Sharon called DoCS straight away: 'I'm telling you she could die if you don't take her off this bloody drug! When she was discharged the doctors said she should be monitored . . . Alambi have never seen her off the drug, how can they monitor anything? We're the only ones who know her . . . sorry? So, you intend to leave her in this state over Christmas? You won't do anything?' Jessie had a follow-up appointment with a paediatrician in Newcastle scheduled in April we were told. The situation could be assessed then.

'In the meantime we are following the discharge documents,' DoCS said repeatedly without even laying eyes on her.

Sharon kept at it but her phone calls and emails made no impact. We watched Jessie suffer and deteriorate steadily in the ten days following her hospital discharge waiting for a recovery that never came. By New Year's Eve it was no longer a question of 'developing a tolerance' after nearly four weeks on the drug. To leave her like this for another *three and a half months* was unconscionable.

We were compelled to act; the ship was clearly rudder-less and the skipper wasn't even on board. So in desperation, as soon as possible after New Year's Eve, we took Jessie to our GP, Dr Baker. Because he knew her he could see she was over-sedated and unhesitatingly recommended the dose be halved immediately, and then halved again after three days if she still appeared to be having trouble. We had to wait as DoCS checked with Legal. To everyone's surprise they discovered that we, the parents, had authority to make this decision with medical back-up all along.

What chilled us is the question: what might have happened to Jessie had we not been there? Could she have become yet another tragic statistic?

When the world got back to 'normal' in the first week in January DoCS called us in to iron everything out. I recall this day well. It was a sweltering 40 degrees and Sharon insisted I wear my black double-breasted suit. In the meeting I had to keep my jacket buttoned tightly to hide my sweat-soaked shirt which was plas-tered to my body. We were there to talk things through and work out the best way forward DoCS told us. They wanted to listen to what we had to say. We were heartened. Maybe, just maybe, they were going to bring Jessie back from Newcastle. What else could it be?

We were escorted to a conference room and settled in. At the head of the table sat a pixie-like regional manager with closely-cropped dark hair. She wore a short, black tunic, black stockings and had a swirl of authority.

Suddenly she started speaking as if someone had turned her on. 'DADHC have joined us today to work together in a spirit of collaboration with Jessie's best interests in mind,' she intoned.

'Let's not think of this as something that's fallen between the cracks, let's think of this as an opportunity to build bridges between DADCH, ourselves, and you, the parents, in the best interests of Jessie,' she continued, exchanging warm nods with the others, who were also muttering 'build bridges' and nodding enthusiastically.

But our hopes were quickly dashed. DoCS announced Jessie would stay in Newcastle until a foster family could be found and that this was likely to take a very long time. 'A very long time,' they repeated. 'It's in the best interests of the child.'

My mind was charging. Jessie would be in Newcastle indefinitely! Finally I spoke: 'Surely it would be better to bring Jessie back to Sydney . . .'

The manager changed the subject: 'Regarding contact, I don't think it's in Jessie's best interest to be travelling to and from Newcastle three weekends a month.' Sharon looked up, disbelief flooding her face, hand suspended in mid-air clasping her pen, about to speak. They were trying to reduce our access to Jessie!

'Actually Jessie loves travelling more than anything,' I quickly interceded. 'She just loves it. Queensland in a day is not too far. It's a peculiarity of her condition. If she finds the car unlocked . . .'

And so it continued. Every point or suggestion I raised was dismissed; DoCS had to act 'in the best interests of the child' and we just didn't understand. But in truth our understanding was growing by the minute. This manager didn't know who Jessie was and never would. None of them ever would. A month had gone by and not one of them had yet met her. Sharon was furious the manager didn't even know Jessie had been moved to a new Allambi house; she didn't know of course because Jessie wasn't *her* child. That was the point. Too many children, a chronic shortage of fosterers, no accommodation and a system that ravenously demanded convoluted process was the nightmare these people faced daily and it seemed they stayed at arm's length from it rather than go mad.

But Jessie's welfare was at stake and the discussion became fraught between Sharon and the manager. Sharon weighed in with a string of hard questions and it emerged that Allambi was being paid a scandalous King's ransom to look after Jessie—$11,000 A WEEK—when we could get no assistance at all. 'The system is not perfect,' the manager confessed.

Sharon asked what the manager knew about Jessie's illness. The manager counter-punched fiercely: 'We will continue to be advised by the medical experts, as should you!'

Sharon then reached over the table, looking steadily into the manager's eyes. 'But the medical experts said to monitor Jessie over Christmas. For God's sake, she was half dead and Allambi called her "lethargic"! And what about these so-called specialist carers you talked about? You told us the only people who could offer Jessie the specialist care she required was this placement in Newcastle, 160 kilometres away. The girls looking after Jessie have an average age of 20, some have no experience at all, and they change so often I can't keep up with who is who. Is that what you call specialised care? They don't even know how to change her hearing aids!' Sharon, a mother protecting her child, was becoming so upset I thought I might have to step in. 'Now we hear you don't even know where she's living!' she cried.

But I have to give DoCS credit—they listened to us after a fashion, and the meeting did achieve something. Within a day they wrote announcing that a new spirit of collaboration would prevail between us. The 'misunderstandings' of the past were instructive about a new way forward. Ours was not a risk-of-harm issue, and we could all work together in the best interests of the child. 'Jessie's parents will be actively involved,' they said, and 'decisions will be made collaboratively.' Most issues could be decided by Allambi and ourselves, and DoCS would only need to become involved if there was disagreement. DoCS also abandoned their attempt to limit our contact with Jessie. We were delighted.

Two days later on 6 January the 'spirit of collaboration' came into play for the first time. Jessie's three-day trial on a halved dose of risperidone had expired and Allambi agreed she was still hopelessly over-sedated. They agreed further to reduce the risperidone dose immediately, precisely as Dr Baker had instructed in writing. It was a Saturday so we couldn't check with DoCS, but we felt sure they'd be fine with this.

Early the following week DoCS organised a consultation with Dr Simon Brooks, Jessie's paediatrician. This seemed strange, as the new agreement had expressly said that medical appointments should be organised by Allambi and ourselves and only a few days earlier DoCS had been happy to wait until April for a follow-up appointment.

Dr Brooks, kindly and affable, had broken the news that Jessie had a genetic condition before referring us to geneticist, Dr Hay. Dr Brooks normally took his time in consultations like the family doctors of yesteryear, but this day was different. Before I could open my mouth he spoke, his eyes on the Allambi manager. 'So you reduced risperidone to a quarter,' he said as the manager nodded sheepishly. I wondered how on earth he had this information as no-one had yet spoken.

Dr Brooks then looked at us, leant forward and announced:

197

'Jessie will remain on this drug, and when her tolerance grows it will be increased!' Sharon, who was about to speak, closed her mouth, stunned.

The DoCS worker attending the consultation then smirked. It was quick and fleeting, but it lingered long enough for all to see. This image of her adolescent triumph still burns in our minds. Was the medication now nothing to do with Jessie, but a battle between us? Surely not—but why did she gloat like someone who had won a round?

Dr Brooks then lectured Sharon and me sternly about what was in Jessie's best interests in terms of medication. Remarkably, he already knew the risperidone dose had been twice reduced: DoCS had clearly briefed him. Indeed he kept mistakenly calling the DoCS case worker present by her manager's name. Somehow, despite our shared history with Jessie, he'd become convinced we were renegades who would challenge whatever path he and his colleagues recommended.

We were floored. We still hadn't uttered a word.

'Hang on a minute,' said Sharon. 'What if I want her off this drug? I mean, we're meant to have medical control.'

Dr Brooks turned to the DoCS case worker, genuinely shocked. 'I thought you had medical control,' he said, totally confused.

'No . . . no,' she stuttered. 'In cases where . . . in cases where there is a difference of opinion, we will take it to the Children's Guardian. It's in the best interests of the child.'

'Oh, yes,' nodded Dr Brooks, realising he'd been suckered, 'the best interest of the child.'

This was a real shock. What was it all about? In retrospect I think DoCS had become convinced we would try to get Jessie off risperidone completely, and they thought that chopping and changing this drug, off and on, would be very bad for her. Sharon had confessed to them that she withheld the drug the night before we saw Dr Baker, feeling she had no choice. Whatever the case, the much lauded spirit of collaboration didn't last a week.

DoCS just couldn't let go and now they firmly regained total 'control'. Our access to Jessie was reduced in petty fashion—two out of every three weekends instead of three out of every four. Medical appointments were missed or neglected. She went without hearing aids for three months when she had only six months to a year left to learn new words and skills.

DoCS inhabited a world overwhelmed by crises every single day. In this circumstance it is unsurprising that the general administration of Jessie's life languished.

Two months later Fran and Maree dropped in to see us together. 'I pleaded with them,' said Maree, who'd taken it upon herself to contact DoCS and offer her expertise on the most appropriate school for Jessie in Newcastle. 'I even suggested contacting the principals for them, but they just didn't want to know. And they talk about the best interests of the child. Unbelievable. Anyway, she must have settled in some time ago by now.'

'Actually, they told us this morning she started school two weeks ago at Lakeside,' I said.

'She's been in school for two weeks and nobody told you!' exclaimed Fran, spluttering coffee down her white shirt. Fran too had been ringing and ringing and leaving messages. When she finally got through to DoCS they were so rude and dismissive it made her blood boil.

'She didn't start until Week five . . .' said Maree shaking her head. 'That's over half the term, and the child might have less than a year to learn! Unbelievable!'

A door started banging upstairs and Sharon charged off to batten it down. When I told them only one kid in Jessie's class was verbal Maree put her head in her hands and started shaking.

'We've got to get up there, Maree,' Fran said.

Sharon came back holding an email, looking dejected and lost. She read it out loud. 'As you are aware, Ms Tess Cunningham (pseudonym) contacted me this morning regarding arranging a visit to Jessie in her placement at Newcastle. After discussing this with casework manager, Trudie Bennett (pseudonym), and Acting manager client services, Katrina Shaw (pseudonym), it was agreed that due to a large amount of people already involved with Jessie in Newcastle it would not be . . . ' and here Sharon paused for emphasis, 'in her best interests to have more people visit this location at this stage.'

'Fuck them!' I exploded. 'The only people Jessie sees apart from her carers are three DADHC workers who visit for an hour once a month! It's one thing to blunder and grope around in the dark . . . but this . . . this is just bloody-mindedness. They're trying to fuck us over but they're fucking Jessie over while they're at it.'

I said some other stuff too but I'll spare you that. Fran and Maree understood my pain and didn't mind the language one little bit.

It felt as if no simple request could be granted now. It felt as if Jessie would stay in Newcastle forever. Did DoCS suspect Jessie's teachers of being spies working in collusion with us, the 'troublemakers'? I've tried hard to make sense of the way they shut out Jessie's teachers but I can't. Whichever way I look at it I can only conclude that Jessie's 'best interests' were not part of their thinking. Maybe they thought we were always trying to manoeuvre them and they had to counter-manoeuvre; maybe they thought we had pushed them into a political dance. Sadly such thinking reflected their own world, not ours.

As the months drifted by Jessie seemed to become more and more entrenched in Newcastle. We felt defeated and powerless. Sharon looked smaller, less robust and had lost a lot of weight. Her once rosy, chubby-cheeked face now had a gaunt, sallow, haunted look. If someone asked her how she was going, in that off-the-cuff way one has when they don't really want an answer, she would cry. If I went to the toilet in the early hours of the morning I would find her sitting on the lounge: a tiny, childlike figure curled up in the chair. She had hit rock bottom, she could get no lower. My heart ached to help but I too was fragile.

But it wasn't all doom and gloom. Since starting school at Lakeside in Newcastle Jessie was definitely recovering from the over-medication, albeit slowly. A few of the words she'd lost were coming back and she was much more animated and lively during the day. The strict regime and the care and attention from round-the-clock dedicated carers at the Allambi house was helping too and she was starting to sleep again.

Now she was stable on the lower dose she was having fun too, jumping on the trampoline, going down the slide and skidding down the path on her tricycle, cheering all the way. She was coming back to her old self and my heart filled with sweet joy. Sometimes she seemed upset when we parted now but it was fleeting; gone by the time the car had backed out of the driveway. Actually I was heartened by this, it was another sign she was returning to the land of the living. My spirits further lifted one night when a simple email turned our world around.

'Sharon, read this, they've replied already! I only sent it this morning!' I shouted excitedly, running down the stairs. I watched the colour return to my beautiful wife's face. It was an email from a stranger, Mary Lou Carter, the party secretary of the Carers Alliance, a new political party that had almost prevailed in the 2007 Senate election.

> What DADHC and DoCS have done to you is absolutely abominable. They use the love that you have for your child as a weapon against you to say nothing of what they have done to Jessie.
>
> There is a philosophy that disabled children should be with their families—full-stop—it is a perversion of the human rights of families and the person with a disability. What good is it to anyone if the family disintegrates completely? DADHC and DoCS are cumbersome, over-bureaucratised organisations with too many managers who really are not across the need for flexible, responsive services that meet the very high support needs of families caring for a disabled child . . . without support and services families faced with catastrophic circumstances, such as that which afflict your dear sweet Jessie, cannot survive.

Mary Lou showed us we were not alone: that we weren't weak or uncaring. Perhaps, along with Jessie, we were victims too who simply couldn't cope when the system demanded we fight our battle in the home, alone. Mary Lou showed us that others saw what we saw, and felt what we felt. It was wrong. It needed to be changed. She wanted to visit. Sharon and I didn't say anything, we didn't need to. We both knew the fight was on, head-on.

CHAPTER 19

HEAD-ON
Sharon

Thursday 3rd January 2008
Please forgive us, Jessie. If you only knew the love we feel. You
are not with Mummy and Daddy at the moment, little one,
but you are with us every minute of the day. In all that we do,
you are the drive and we WILL make this right.

Let me take you back in time before the email from Mary Lou.
There is much we have left out, some of it too unbearable to
revisit. Being forced to relinquish your child through lack of
services is heinous and we vowed to fight this injustice. Not just
for ourselves and Jessie, but for the many others who couldn't—
be it from fatigue, not knowing how to, or more tragically, from
fear of public opinion. In an early meeting with DoCS and their
managers I vowed to them: 'If you don't intend to bring Jessie
back to Sydney, you leave us no option. We will mount a media

campaign bigger than anything you have ever seen and believe me, we will never stop.'

So begins this part of the story.

'Trust me!' said Michelle Cazzulino as she briskly strode from our house, photographers in tow. Trust a journalist? I'd worked with them, knew how the sniff of a particular angle could often elbow out the truth—but there had been a look in Michelle's eyes.

When Jessie went into DoCS' care, Stuart, in a flurry to get media attention, had called on all he knew: journos, TV and radio friends, publicists—no stone was left unturned. Within two days *Daily Telegraph* reporter, Michelle Cazzulino, was at our door. Toughened from years of reporting on the mean streets of London she maintained a detached air, but later confided that ours was one of the most harrowing tales she'd ever heard.

When the story came out we spent the entire day on the phone or bashing on our computers, urging friends, family, acquaintances and those we hardly knew to write to the *Telegraph*'s editor and to ask their friends to do the same. I even compiled ideas on what they might write. The response was amazing.

Virtual strangers wrote back with a copy of the letter they'd submitted. Some said they'd forwarded my email to 50 friends who were also sending it on to another 50; all would write a letter. There was outrage and sorrow and the *Telegraph* must have been blitzed with hundreds of letters in the end.

But only one or two were published days later, and our story sank like a stone.

'Stuart,' I mumbled, nudging the inert body beside me. It was dark and I couldn't see but there were fifty ideas swimming in my head. According to Stuart my mind is triply active compared to the average person and when an idea comes I have to share it. It doesn't matter if Stuart's in the shower, on the loo or in deep concentration playing his favourite piece of music—when the idea comes it's to be grabbed there and then. It especially happens first thing in the morning, so he tells me. But having wriggled to the far edge of the bed away from my poking finger, and still snoring loudly, Stuart's gaping mouth signalled: 'Do something else with your ideas'.

Downstairs I surveyed the notes I'd made the night before. I'm always the one taking notes and throwing out ideas. This sponsors a new thought in Stuart's head, which formulates yet another in mine—and so it goes. I'm the catalyst, but his execution invariably surpasses my original push, and as I added more ideas I thought, 'The poor bloke doesn't need respite from Jessie, he needs respite from me'.

At the top of the page I'd written in larger-than-required, capital letters framed by asterixes: PRINT—RADIO—TV. 'I should be exhausted,' I thought, 'but all I wanted was for Stuart to wake up so we could start again.'

'Hi, Sis.' My brother Terry was standing in the kitchen smiling, with a beaming Bi Bi in his arms, his white English legs tormenting my eyes as they reflected the glare of the bright morning sun.

'It's not a good time, Terry,' I'd said when he'd announced he was coming over from the UK.

'I'm not coming for a holiday,' he retorted, 'I'm coming to help.' He's a chirpy soul, my brother but I wasn't in the mood for being cheered up. As it turned out his help proved invaluable as he was able to care for Bi Bi, leaving Stuart and me free to drum up media interest. Bi Bi, like Terry, was a never-ending joker and each day off they would go on some exciting new adventure.

Differing descriptions of Bi Bi's personality by the orphanage in China had led us to assume they weren't sure who she was. However, back in Australia, this child's personality was unmistakable. Bi Bi was a loud, robust, natural entertainer. Her latest trick was to skid across the floor of the corner shop, come to an abrupt halt and yell: 'Hel-lo baby!' in a deep husky, mischievous voice to Steve, the owner. After scoring the desired chocolate, she would turn to Steve, raise her thumb and whisper in conspiratorial glee: 'Magic!' She also showed a natural talent for somersaulting, whether into her cot at night or around the garden—she somersaulted over anything in her way. This exhibitionism led many to assume her birth parents were gymnasts—Stuart and I thought circus acrobats or clowns more likely.

But with Jessie she was soft. One time when Jessie was down from Newcastle for the weekend, I recall being on the phone to a journalist from *Notebook* magazine. Jessie was trying hard to get a removable plastic chair leg back into its hole. Bi Bi, squatting in the sidelines, was itching to take over and eventually Jessie's slow, unsuccessful bumbling was too much: snatching the leg, she put it straight in the hole with a triumphant grin. Jessie was crestfallen and I was about to say something when Bi Bi, who must have seen the look also, took out the leg, gave it to Jessie and gently showed her how to put it back in. Episodes like this touched both our hearts. Bi Bi had spent three years of her life in a survival-of-the-fittest world. Here she was slowly thawing out, warmed by the love all around her, and for the first time in her life able to give it back. Bi Bi was a life tonic, and despite our sadness and despondency she brought a magical beauty to our lives.

'I'm just going up to work on the submission,' I said to Terry and, kissing Bi Bi, scurried up the stairs, keeping one ear out for the sleepy bastard in the next room who was now fit to wake the dead with his trumpeting snores.

Commissioner James Wood QC, a man of impressive reputation, was heading a new inquiry into all aspects of child protection, and submissions from the public had been invited. There had been too many headlines on children who had died whilst known to DoCS. The public wanted answers and the state government couldn't tread water any longer.

Neither of us had much hope our submission would change anything, but at least if we wrote it well, it might be taken seriously. We put our heart and soul into that submission and spent night after night, weekend after weekend, chained to our computers perfecting it. 'We'll get the final draft edited by a professional,' said Stuart in book publisher mode. 'Jessie's happiness and future is at stake.'

'What time is it?' Stuart was standing by the door wiping his eyes, his hair standing on end like the man on the film poster of David Lynch's *Eraserhead*. When Jessie was taken into care, Stuart's hair took a peculiar turn: it just wouldn't stay down. He looked permanently like he'd had an electric shock. Nothing could get it to lay flat. He would emerge from the shower with it combed close to his head and by mid-morning it was standing like stalks. Like many men he is not easily given to displays of emotion and in this case his hair was doing it for him.

Before I could fire one of the fifty ideas at him the phone went. 'If it's the media, focus on the medication,' I shot out as I ran down the stairs, taking the phone and thrusting it at Stuart, who was still in the land of Nod. 'Who is it?' I mouthed as Stuart waved me off, moving back up the stairs to his office. Scurrying up after him I listened to him recounting the story for the fifty-seventh time and worked out it was a producer from the ABC's *7.30 Report*. Beside myself with excitement, lest he leave anything out, I was making notes and thrusting them in front of him, elbowing him to pay attention, and with a rapid ding, ding, ding of my finger on the paper showing him exactly where to look.

This was how all calls would go. 'Sorry, what was that?' Stuart would say, trying to ward me off. When no pen was available I'd be mouthing the words to him full in his face. Stuart would interrupt the call, place his hand over the phone and turn to me: 'What?'

Day in, day out we worked, often well into the evening. Stuart worried we'd become obsessive. The idea worried me also. Some time previously, when he launched a book on whistle-blowers we'd both seen obsessed people, people who were so eaten up by their predicament it left them slightly mad.

And in between—as madness can take you—we would laugh and sing and joke with Bi Bi with boundless energy, teaching her to get our dog, Magnus, to howl. There would be early mornings at 4 a.m. with Jessie, on a home visit, running up and down the corridor, unable to sleep. As she screamed and laughed and careered around we would be writing notes, talking endless strategy. At weekends, before Bi Bi and Jessie went to bed, the whole household would be going. Magnus would be howling, with both children howling too. Stuart would be on his guitar singing, Terry would be trying to tell a joke, I would be dancing, Bi Bi would be somersaulting over the floor, jumping to attention and tumbling again; Jessie, banging everything she could see. Neither Jessie nor Magnus knew what was going on—Magnus at 13 was approaching senility and Jessie, well . . . Jessie was Jessie. Neither could hear but the energy brought them to a frenzy.

Mary Lou Carter from the Carers Alliance swept into our lives with the force of a twister. Mary Lou has her own troubles. Her intellectually disabled son, a strapping 17-year-old of rugby proportions, who has been known to throw her against walls, attended Kingsdene Special School; the only boarding school in NSW for intellectually disabled children. Soon his time there would be up and with nowhere for him to go, he would again be in her sole care. But despite her personal problems she took on our cause with the energy and ferocity of a mother magpie: constantly busy, constantly darting, always with one eye on her babies.

'Nell,' she barked down the phone, mouthing to us conspiratorially that Nell was the assistant of the shadow minister, Andrew Constance. 'I have the Neals here. We need to see Andrew immediately.'

'Steady on!' I wanted to whisper. But Mary Lou was shrieking down the phone, 'Next week isn't good enough, Nell. I don't care. Of course it's outrageous.' She carried on like this, indignant and demanding, and I felt sure our hopes of ever seeing the shadow minister were dead. 'How are you placed this afternoon?' she asked as she crisply snapped the phone shut.

'Is it okay to give Bi Bi crisps?' Bi Bi, who had starved in the orphanage, was completely silenced by food. Andrew Constance, the NSW Shadow Minister for Ageing, Disability and Home Care smiled.

Months before, our local member gave us 15 minutes of his time. Today Andrew spent the entire afternoon listening to our story, thoughtfully trying to work out a plan to assist. We told him that our local member's letters insisting the family was in crisis had been ignored by both DADHC and DoCS ministers. We showed him the 'before' and 'after' photos of Jessie, which graphically portrayed the risperidone medication fiasco, and he was genuinely disgusted.

'Jessie could be back in Sydney today,' he muttered angrily. 'One phone call from the Minister, that's all it would take.' Andrew would contact the DADHC and DoCS' ministers' press secretaries regarding their lack of response. He would also contact the shadow minister for DoCS and together they would make a strategy. He would do his best to garner media interest.

Looking down I noticed Bi Bi eating crisps from Andrew's shoe. She had made his office into a massive picnic ground and was now ensuring no crumb was wasted. 'It's okay, I've got a child,' said Andrew.

'Not one like Bi Bi,' I thought: 'She's a veritable vacuum cleaner where food is concerned!'

Andrew was unlike any politician I'd ever seen—he was sincere. He delayed his long drive home to Bega by several hours and graciously missed dinner with his young family that day, just for us. He employed his assistant, Nell, because she had a 21-year-old disabled daughter, knowing that in order to fully understand his disability portfolio he needed to be closer to the difficulties families faced and knowing compromises would be necessary to enable Nell to take on both roles.

'Why's he doing all this for us?' I asked Stuart as we walked back to the car, little Bi Bi bouncing between us with a bulbous stomach. 'What's in it for him?'

'Cases like ours give the Opposition an opportunity to attack those in power. It's also a way to make a name for himself—but I agree with you, he's unusual. I think he actually cares,' said Stuart, bundling a farting Bi Bi into her baby seat.

The next morning our local member's office rang. Both DoCS and DADHC ministers had responded to our letters. We had waited months, had written follow-up letters, yet one phone call made late in the afternoon from Andrew Constance had prompted an overnight reply.

'It's what I expected,' Andrew told Stuart over the phone, discussing the 'we're not involved' letter from the Minister for Disabilities, and the disinterested 'whitewash' from the Minister for Community Services' staff. He wanted us to counter their claims.

I felt a depressing realisation. I thought these agencies would jump into action, but they fobbed off Andrew just as dismissively as us and with such gall. My hopes of having this situation resolved in a couple of weeks were dashed.

Jessie was still incredibly skinny following her recent medication upheaval and her gait was more awkward due to her right foot turning in. I shook the reason for this out of my head and watched. On her head was a turquoise sunhat and her left trouser leg was idiosyncratically pulled up to the knee. She was bent in concentration, walking backwards and forwards clearing condiments one at a time from the table, oblivious of Bi Bi who, arms out like a defender in netball, was trying to prevent her passing.

I missed Jessie's laughter. A joyous moment for Jessie explodes unpredictably, out of nothing, and cascades into bursts of giggling at something only she can see. Such moments are uplifting for all to witness—Jessie's joy is their joy because what they see is a startling purity; someone totally untainted by ego and the socialisation that infects the rest of us.

Having thrown several of the condiments into the bin, Jessie

with serious self-importance was back to the dining table looking for more action. Suddenly my unfinished plate was whipped
out from under me, the fork flying missile-like, bang into the
wall. I burst out laughing and reached out to touch her. Blank-
faced, she pulled away. It was piercing. Jessie, who only a year
earlier had been at my heels constantly, pushing Stuart out of
the way to get to me, now recoiled when I approached her.

'She won't come near me!' I said to Stuart as Jessie ran
towards him.

'She doesn't know who you are,' he replied, picking her up,
inferring the effect of over-medication. I said nothing but was
painfully aware how she clung only to him night and day. I was
also painfully aware of the real reason. Deep within me I believed
Jessie felt I'd abandoned her. It overwhelmed me because I felt
she was right. So when she came home and ignored me, I kept my
distance—it broke my heart, but I deserved the cold shoulder.

Days turned into weeks, Terry returned to the UK, and the weeks
turned into months, yet on we fought with anger and grief as
our constant companions. As the summer sunshine streamed
full blast outside we were holed up in the house, typing or on
the phones in an obsessive charge to bring attention to the gross
injustice of our situation, in between battling DoCS and the fact
our daughter was dying.

The Wood Commission, media friends and publicists,
ministers, local members, federal MPs, Carers Alliance, former
DoCS mates, disability organisations, *7.30 Report*, *Daily Telegraph*, producers of *Australian Story*, the *Today* show, *Notebook*,
Sydney Morning Herald, *Australian*—we went through them all.

But as Jessie remained in Newcastle and no-one interceded,
reality set in. We were just another story in the paper. As time

passed, the *7.30 Report* lost interest and, bit by bit, everything fell away and came to nothing.

Humiliating flashbacks recalling my audacious claims to DoCS in early January haunted me. I shuddered as I saw myself leaning back in the chair, dramatically announcing how we'd pulverise them with a media campaign. I wished I'd never said it and felt like a fool. We realised now that the media wasn't interested in disability stories unless there's the drama of death, torture and paedophilia. And as there was plenty of that about, the competition was fierce.

We were also running out of time. Our temporary care agreement was for six months and couldn't be extended. It was due to run out in June 2008. After that, the case would go to court and Jessie would be made a ward of the state, with our rights as parents removed and DoCS in control to do as they saw fit. It was incomprehensible that out-of-home care was not available to parents who loved their child, but if the parents 'neglected' their child, that facility was readily available. The madness of it all was sending me demented because now we had only eight weeks left. Eight weeks! We had been fighting for four months, only to get nowhere. What could we do in eight weeks? Who could we turn to, what could we do? When Stuart started talking about getting a good lawyer, a frantic panic swelled and a heavy, dark veil of depression descended.

It was also during this time that Stuart was made redundant. While the redundancy was not unwanted, it was totally unexpected—and no matter how we rationalised, it was another blow.

It was a bleak, wretched time—the misery compounded by DoCS, who continued unabated, burrowing into every crevice of our world with bullying, supercilious arrogance.

Around this time I asked a friend to come in and look after

Bi Bi. I couldn't get out of bed and Stuart couldn't function. We had been allowed just over two days in every three weeks with Jessie and even this was being further eroded. 'How can they get away with it?' I moaned to Stuart. Neither of us could face dealing with DoCS directly again. We needed an advocate who could speak for Jessie, but like everything else our dogged search for that came to nothing.

We had no more people to contact; nowhere else to go. We had tried everything and failed.

CHAPTER 20

VOYAGE TO ITHACA

Sharon

'You've lost your fight.'

My new psychologist, a small-boned, tiny Greek woman with Angelina Jolie lips, was peering quizzically over her glasses, probing. The past months had brought me to my knees and I was at a complete loss as to how to cope.

'At the beginning of the year, when I first saw you, you were ready to take on the world. You were going to fight for all those who couldn't.'

She was right. Back then I'd been outraged by what we had gone through, what others go through, what Jessie had gone through; back then I'd hoped we could change things. Now I felt crumpled, hopeless and broken—even Jessie wanted nothing to do with me.

'Guilt's got in your way,' she said with a penetrating gaze. I looked up at her, searching her eyes for answers—why *shouldn't*

I feel guilty? I who stood by mutely as carers took my small, terrified, crying child out of our house, out of her home to a frightening world of strangers a two-hour drive away. What sort of mother was I who stood there and let them? Why didn't I rescue her?

'You need to learn to self-soothe,' she said with a gentle lilt. 'Oh God,' I thought, 'where's this going?' I nodded, adjusting my skirt, trying to look like I was seriously with her.

As if she'd read my thoughts, the psychologist smiled, then leant towards me, her voice almost a whisper: 'What would you say to someone in your situation, Sharon?' Her eyes were twinkling as she studied my face, waiting for understanding.

'I'd say you're not doing your child a favour by keeping them in a situation where you find each day unbearable. What sort of environment is that for a child? I'd say I understand how hard it must be, but if you sacrifice your life, what will it do to your family, what will it do to the child? It's not your fault you can't cope.' It came out before I could even think: such a fluent rationale untainted by the complexities of love. The understanding hit me like a thunderbolt.

'Your journey reminds me of Odysseus's fight to get home to Ithaca. Everywhere Odysseus turned there were unimaginable obstacles. Only through his guile, intelligence and resourcefulness was he able to overcome them. This is your journey. At each turn there is a battle. Guilt is your battle, but you have to fight it. There are bigger battles: fight for your rights, your family's rights and for all those who aren't able to fight.'

It was so clear, so simple and in that moment I understood. The feelings of guilt, the fear that people were judging me for not keeping Jessie, the intense pain of separation, feeling demoralised by DoCS—my inner battle was destroying me and I was ignoring the real battle, the one I really needed to fight. To be forced to abandon your child in order to get help was wrong. It was wrong and that was unacceptable.

With renewed energy—and after finding out the story of Odysseus from Stuart—I vowed we would take on the sweet-voiced Sirens, the gigantic, one-eyed Cyclops and anything else in our way. 'So what if we're obsessive,' I said to him. 'Don't fight it, Stuart, rejoice in it because this obsession is the fuel we need to keep going.' And so, with resolve in our hearts, like Odysseus, we became resourceful and searched for fresh ways to reach our goal.

But something else tugged at my soul, and with Odysseus in mind it took precedence above all else.

When Jessie came rocketing into the house the following Saturday, I grabbed her, tussling with her. When she tried to wriggle out of my arms I pulled her to me with a force I didn't know I had and kissed her. I kissed her hair; I kissed her hands and told Stuart to pick up Bi Bi who was clambering in between us. I ignored the Allambi carer waiting for me to make her usual cup of tea. Instead, I put on the Chinese DVD Jessie and I used to watch day after day not so long ago. When she tried to get away, I tackled her back onto the sofa, stroking her hair and holding her tight like I used to.

The familiar lilting pipes so distinctive of Chinese music bounced from the TV. This DVD had always thrilled and delighted Jessie and that thrilled me. With the music on, I now danced like I used to in front of her, executing all manner of enthusiastic gyrations, ignoring the incredulous stares of the Allambi worker who hurriedly trotted into the kitchen. My focus was on Jessie. I remembered how Jessie, with pursed lips, would smile to herself, look at me and burst out giggling when I used to do this. I remembered how she would put her face close to mine and peer into my eyes with incredible intensity. She was still blank-faced, but at least now she wasn't trying to get away. She was watching me. I joined in with the presenter, pointing to my head: 'Tóu', then to my nose: 'Bízi'; theatrically pronouncing each of the words as they did. I sat with her the entire show. I had attention on one thing only—you are my daughter, I love you and you are going to know it!

I realised that as Jessie was older, taller and heavier than Bi Bi, Stuart and I had naturally assumed the caring role of he to the heavy, me to the small. 'No more,' I said to him. 'From now on I change Jessie, I dress her, take her out of the bath.' And so I did. I kissed her, praised her and slept in the bed with her and, bit by bit, her love came back. Jessie seemed as surprised as I, and I realised that allowing her to ignore me had been a vicious circle.

I knew also that a year ago, when I had been on my knees from exhaustion and despair at the relentlessness of caring for her, that I had pulled away. 'You do it now,' I had said to Stuart when he took long service leave. 'I can't bear it anymore!'

Now that we'd had respite I could breathe again. Refreshed, I was able to love my child with the vigour and intensity of the past. When finally Jessie scrambled over Stuart to get to me, headbutting me in the face in an attempt to kiss my lips, I felt a fierce protective love engulf my soul.

'One more battle fought—a battle won,' I thought. And one of the sweetest, for now I had my baby back.

But the other battle lay ahead: how to bring attention to Jessie's plight? Stuart consulted a lawyer he knew who worked in the area of disabilities. Her one word of advice had been: 'Escalate'.

It didn't matter who we contacted, we needed to bring all guns in, and this became our sole focus.

We also needed a press release so a friend put us in contact with her brother, Rod Campbell, a Canberra-based journalist. In great detail he outlined the central principles of an effective press release and then wrote a brilliant draft one for us. The time and effort he invested and the care and compassion which shone from his words had even Stuart on the verge of tears. Rod died of lung cancer two months later. It was a great shock. This stranger's attempt to help our little girl secure a better life while his own was painfully ebbing away is one of the most selfless acts I have ever known.

With little time remaining, we became tenacious. Stuart spent days on the phone to various advocacy and disability groups. I made speeches at disability playgroups inciting mothers to stand up and be counted. We got hordes of people to write to their local member and contact parliamentarians they knew personally. We appealed to Bill Shorten, the federal Parliamentary Secretary for Disabilities and Children's Services, for help. The fact that he never replied did not deter us. We wrote to DoCS' complaints department with little hope this would achieve much, but as simply one more way to escalate. Finally, on the brink of approaching *A Current Affair*, *Today Tonight* and *60 Minutes* we made a list of producers, people who might know them, and also wrote a media release. It was a bit risky since you never know how 'tabloid TV' will present a story, but we now had nothing to lose.

We also contacted Andrew Constance's office again. They were still appalled by Jessie's placement in another city and were keen to remain involved. Andrew wanted to table questions in Parliament, so for days we fed Nell information. Nell got so carried away she formulated hundreds of questions that had to be pulled back. Their incredible care and interest in Jessie's welfare moved us deeply. Through Andrew's office we were also in contact with the Shadow Minister for Community Services, Katrina Hodgkinson, and spent days liaising with her on further questions for Parliament. It was a giddy time of 'race against the clock' and though we knew the court case where Jessie would be made a ward of the state was inevitable, we hoped that any presiding magistrate would have an awareness of the situation and be empathetic.

'Will it make a difference? I mean the Ombudsman's a bit of a toothless tiger . . .' I was hurrying to get to work.

'The more people we get involved, the more we escalate,' replied Stuart. I stared at him, put down my bag, picked up the phone and spoke to Margo Barton from the Ombudsman's office. I have no idea what I said but amidst hopeless weeping was one core plea: 'Help us; they've placed our child in another city. This is wrong.'

Finally, questions on Jessie's behalf were being asked in Parliament and many more were tabled. The ministers would have around 30 days to respond. Nell was also chasing Adele Horin from the *Sydney Morning Herald* on our behalf.

'Sharon, have you seen this?' It was Stuart from the next room.

'I'm trying to concentrate!' I answered, agitated. I was uptight striving for hooks to tempt Adele. We needed this story.

'I think you should read this,' said Stuart now standing by my office door, holding up an email, a bemused look on his face.

Gail Furness, Counsel Assisting Justice Wood, wanted permission to use extracts of our submission for discussion at the Inquiry's public forum that Friday. It would be sent to DoCS and DADHC's most senior management to discuss shortfalls in their systems.

'Oh my God, I don't believe this! Stuart, Stuart!' I squealed, jumping up and down, throwing myself into his arms, sending him stumbling and tumbling within an inch of the stairs. In a flash I was back at my computer relaying this development to Adele Horin, knowing this was the hook we needed. She was in our lounge room with a photographer the next day and her story—'How policy forced a family to desert their child'—ran on page three of the *Herald* on the morning of the public forum.

DoCS and DADHC have always been very adept at justifying their position, which shows how often they are forced to do it. But on Friday 11th April 2008 Commissioner James Wood and Gail Furness were shrewd, hard-hitting and unrelenting.

'We'll turn now to the case of Jessie,' said Commissioner Wood. Stuart gasped. Neither of us thought they would name Jessie! This submission, said Commissioner Wood with a sorry, disparaging shake of his head, epitomised too many stories he had read. He wanted answers so he could understand.

DADHC was under the microscope. How did Jessie end up in DoCS' care? 'I don't feel it's appropriate to talk about this case without the permission of the parents,' said one of the DADHC representatives, shifting in her seat, under pressure.

'She has it!' I shouted, waving my arms at Gail Furness.

'You have their permission,' said Gail with a fleeting wry smile in my direction.

Without a shield, the DADHC managers stumbled and stuttered and scrambled for statistics, muttering words that were hard to follow.

Frustrated, Gail Furness leant forward and peered at them. 'Do you accept that there is a problem as illustrated by the Jessie Neal case and that something needs to be done? Because I don't understand, from what either of you have said so far, that there is an acceptance that there is a problem.'

Once more DADHC went round and round in circles. Judging by the faces in the room I wasn't the only one who felt the excruciating embarrassment of these two executives as they drowned in their own poor show that day.

At last Justice Wood asked if members of the audience wanted to speak. Before others had time to put up their hands I was on my feet, waving, pulling Stuart with me. I would have been dragged out screaming had we been denied. Jessie's future was at stake: the temporary care agreement now only had days to run.

Stuart's voice quivered as he delivered the speech I'd written to a hushed crowd. 'We are the parents of Jessie Neal,' he said softly. He asked how DADHC could maintain a policy preventing out-of-home care for children under 12 no matter what state of crisis the family was in, yet readily report that family to DoCS to get help. He asked how $11,000 spent per week on one child could be justified when hundreds of families scramble to get nothing. Lastly, he wanted to know why DADHC said they would provide a foster family with unlimited support yet we, the actual family, were given none.

It was tender in places, firm in others: a delivery only my gentle husband could have dispensed. When he finished he folded the paper and slowly raised his head; only I saw the tears that glistened in his eyes. Suddenly the room erupted and we were swamped by people. Among the throng were radio journos who, thanks to Adele Horin's article, had covered the Inquiry.

The radio story ran all afternoon with my sobbing account fanning its fire. Eventually it was the second lead news story and by evening the NSW Minister for Community Services,

Kevin Greene, was uneasily defending Jessie's placement in Newcastle.

Within an hour of us returning home from the Inquiry, ABC Radio's Simon Marnie rang. Suddenly, after months of fruitless effort, the media was charging like a speeding train. After much debate we agreed my raw emotion had more impact than Stuart's political erudition and I'd just have to get my head around the political nuances for the breakfast interview the next day.

Sitting on the swing chair at 6.30 a.m. I cleared the detritus from my mind and focused on the palm tree that towered above me. Its willowy fronds shivered in the breeze. Chirping birds surveyed the leftover dog food, warily keeping an eye on Atticus, the cat, stock-still in pounce mode, his tail twitching spasmodically. The night sky was lifting and turning blue. 'This is for Jessie,' I thought. Her rusty tricycle lay forlornly on its side. I saw her soaring down the garden path on it, hair flying behind, careering to an abrupt, screeching halt inches from the garage door. I saw her kick the now sad and faded football into the bushes, chasing after it in her woolly little pale-purple dressing gown with rabbit hood. I saw her everywhere—and I focused.

Many people heard the interview. My GP commented on the affecting mix of honest grief and political statement. It was powerful, he said, because it was clear I had no axe to grind. Someone else heard it: a producer from *Four Corners*. Incredibly, one of its investigative journalists, Quentin McDermott, was doing a story, 'In My Shoes', on the lives of carers.

Simultaneously, Andrew Constance tabled over 30 more questions in Parliament regarding Jessie's placement in Newcastle. On the parliamentary website, question after question on Jessie Neal ran down the entire page. Concurrently the Ombudsman's process was also in motion.

'There's a long way to go. We need to keep our eyes on the ball,' cautioned Stuart, who can't resist a sporting analogy. For once I understood exactly what he meant.

A television interview requires absolute silence; even the fridge gets turned off. 'I'll put my car keys inside so we don't forget to turn it back on,' said the tall, gangly soundman, opening the fridge.

'You'll have to take the kids out I'm afraid,' Quentin said to Stuart.

As Stuart wandered down the garden path, kids in tow, the soundman and Quentin were crawling around on their hands and knees trying to silence a persistent drip from our porch with one of our towels.

While trying to be as eloquent as possible, I spent the first 40 minutes crying. The TV crew became so alarmed they called for a rest break. 'Stay focused, keep your eye on the ball,' Stuart had said. Suddenly I was calm, in control and putting my points across cogently. 'You've seen the footage we took of Jessie, stumbling, dribbling, unable to stand—a zombie over-medicated on risperidone. They just refused to do anything about it! Even after the hospital had said she must be monitored very closely, DoCS just decided we were making it up, without even laying eyes on her.' Quentin looked on, horrified.

Abruptly the soundman jerked, his head jolting sharply to the side like a dog that's caught a sniff in the air. At that moment a massive plane descended over our house, obliterating all. The soundman ran out, came back in and ran out a second time— another plane was coming over. 'Are you on the flight path?' Quentin ventured, not wanting the answer. Quiet again and we were away.

'The government's taking carers for a ride . . .' I said, but my eyes were on the garage door out the window. Stuart was coming up the garden path with Jessie shaking her castanets, head down like a bull, heading for the door. Stuart got halfway before he was ushered by the soundman back into the car, out of the garage, relegated to driving the streets once more.

'So tell me about DoCS, what is wrong with DoCS?' Quentin asked, ignoring Magnus who, having lost his mind, was scratching my leg and possibly going to cock his own.

'DoCS! Well . . . yes . . . well, they don't listen . . . they don't listen, do they?' I could hear another plane coming.

'Just ignore it,' said Quentin, the plane's roar drowning the last half of his sentence.

'So they don't listen?' He was leaning forward as if he genuinely thought I might have more to say. Magnus had changed his mind about my leg. He was moving toward Quentin's. I saw everyone wince and unease flicker over Quentin's tightly smiling face as Magnus scuttled towards him. When I put Magnus out the back he scratched at the door. When I put him out the front he barked. In between, the planes continued and once again Stuart, thinking it must be a wrap by now, came back. From a solid two-hour interview I'm surprised they got the six minutes they did.

The story of Jessie's over-medication made the ABC News at 7.00 p.m. as a teaser for the later *Four Corners*. It showed the then minister for DADHC, Kristina Keneally, commenting that Jessie's dose was quite appropriate for a child her age. *Four Corners* juxtaposed her words with home footage of our child lolling hopelessly in the background. The Minister was made to look unsympathetic. I doubt she would have been happy.

The very day after the program aired we met with the Ombudsman for a DoCS and DADHC conciliation meeting.

After *Four Corners* I had to wonder if conciliation was on their minds.

As all parties signed a confidentiality agreement we are unable to discuss what took place in the meeting. However, the next day the Ombudsman, who was anything but a toothless tiger, phoned to say that her office had informed DoCS and DADHC senior management that the Ombudsman would remain 'an interested party' for the next year.

'You two have no idea of the impact you have made,' she told us. 'I think you will find things better from now on.'

'So what happened next?' asked the psychologist perched on her chair, leaning forward with an earnest look and a rather large grin on her face.

'*Eleven* days before we faced court DoCS informed us they were out of the picture and DADHC would take over.' The psychologist gently held her palms together, placed them to her mouth and tilting her head back, heaved an enormous sigh of relief.

'All our rights have been restored,' I continued excitedly. 'The difference in DADHC's attitude is extraordinary. Once they could do nothing, now they can't do enough.'

'And how is little Jessie?'

I smiled because I could hardly believe it myself: 'She's so happy. When she comes home she runs into our house and is really excited, but by the time Sunday comes she's missing all the fun of the workers. I can't tell you how it felt the first time Stuart told me she ran up the steps to get into the Allambi house. I mean all you want is for your child to be happy and . . . We see her every weekend and have unlimited access. The DADHC staff we deal with are wonderful people, they really care about Jessie and are doing everything they can to bring her back to Sydney. Jessie has a psychologist, a speech therapist, an occupational therapist and a case worker and they've even engaged a special-ised psychologist to oversee her transition back to Sydney. She'll be back soon, I know it. All stops are out to find a foster family who can share her care with us, and no matter who they are Jessie has to like them!' I made a face and the psychologist laughed with me.

I paused, my mood reflective and pensive: 'No-one knows how hard it is looking after a child with a severe disability . . . not unless they've done it. In the end you . . .' I stopped. It was hard to say, but it was the truth. 'In the end you resent the child because it's never-ending . . . and what good is that . . . but . . . but . . .' The psychologist put her hand on my arm as I shook the last seven months' memories from my head.

'What else have you learnt?' she asked softly.

'Learnt?' Had I learnt *anything* from this terrible experience apart from how to deal with horrendous pain? She smiled, her eyes willing me to search deep.

'I think I finally understand why they called us brave. You know, there's this expectation in society that if you truly love your child you will look after it no matter how severe the dis-ability and only those people who sacrifice their lives for their child truly love them. It's just so wrong. To leave parents to cope alone using love as a weapon is . . . is criminal . . . I mean caring is a vocation, it suits some people, it's what they want to do, but for many it's the opposite. It's not just an abuse of families, you know, but . . . but of the disabled child as well, because how can any child thrive in an environment that's blown apart? It's taken a long time,' I whispered softly, 'but I've finally learned not to feel guilty.'

I paused but suddenly another thought poured out from somewhere deep inside that surprised even me. 'What I've learnt more than anything,' I said, my voice cracking, 'is . . . I always felt that to love you had to be loved in return, that love can't exist otherwise. I was wrong.'

The psychologist leant forward in her seat.

'I've learnt that I can love profoundly and unconditionally, that I can love someone even though they don't return it or don't know who I am.'

The psychologist reached for a tissue and for the first time in our sessions it wasn't for me. She was nodding, locking me with her eyes, and I found myself nodding too.

'Do we need to make another appointment?' I asked.

The psychologist paused, put some loose papers in a folder and put the folder away. Turning to me with a smile, she raised her eyebrows. 'What do you think?'

'No, I guess not.'

CHAPTER 21

THE PERFECT DAY

Stuart

On Jessie's seventh birthday the sun belted down gloriously in the middle of winter, forcing many into the shade. The sky was totally cloudless and a rich cobalt blue was smeared perfectly and evenly from one horizon to the other. There was no wind to speak of aside from little puffs that fell away moments after they came. At breakfast you could almost hear the hushed exclamations from millions of households throughout Sydney: 'My God, what a beautiful day!'

Eleven months previously DADHC had quickly found a Sydney placement and, a couple of months after that, Jessie was near us again. Through Life without Barriers they'd engaged a full-time foster carer, Cindy, and as the months rolled by, their promise of continuous respite was honoured without a murmer. Now, nearly a year later, the weekends were mostly looked after by a combination of two respite groups and ourselves, while Cindy did the hard yards Monday to Friday during school terms. DADHC told us they didn't want Cindy to burn out, so there was plenty of institutional respite for school holidays too. This begged lots of questions, but that is not my purpose here.

Cindy was keen to host Jessie's birthday at her home at Dolls Point on Botany Bay, just 30 minutes away, and we were thrilled that she wanted to. We were already close, conferring on everything to do with Jessie, meeting up at the regular round of medical appointments and swapping notes whenever Jessie moved between our houses. For nine months Cindy had stuck it out through wild tantrums and returned bouts of sleeplessness.

'How do you do it?' Sharon asked her.

'Sharon, you both have jobs. This is my job,' she said.

Jessie's mind was now almost completely gone, and as each bit had drifted away her fractiousness increased. Her feet had turned in so far she'd developed a pronounced stoop to keep her from falling and, due to the cocktail of drugs that made her ravenous, she was trying to eat every small thing she could see, including the odd crayon.

But her birthday was not a time of sadness. As I watched her lumbering around the backyard squealing with delight I remembered her second birthday, when she thrived in the spotlight, opening her presents, fully aware it was all about her. Then a cold shiver ran through me as I recalled her third birthday, when she withdrew, already overwhelmed by other children. By her fifth only her favourite adults were allowed but she kept to her DVD most of the time, coming alive suddenly when the candlelit cake was produced. She blew out the candles ten times that day—well Sharon did it for her from the side anyway—and then retreated again to her portable DVD player. And now today I couldn't believe my eyes. She was grinning like a Cheshire cat and bending over low in ratchety spasms, laughing with the descending cadence of a crow: 'A-A-A-A-Arrh.' She was in the spotlight again, and loving it, again; at least for the first hour or so, which is a bloody long time when you've got an attention span of several seconds.

Cindy and her partner, Gared, hired a huge jumping castle that swallowed up half the garden. The other kids loved it but Jessie just hovered near the edge and delighted in watching them do what was now beyond her—as if just having them near was all she needed. On the back porch countless close-up photos of Jessie sleeping, laughing or at play with Cindy, Gared and Cindy's daughter, Christie, were taped around the walls. And from the start, all eyes were on Jessie. When she passed, conversation stopped and a sea of hands shot out to pat her or steady her. The love and warmth from Cindy's family and friends matched the Indian summer day and blew us away. And when Cindy excitedly produced a massive Elmo birthday cake, her tender delight in Jessie, with Gared just a half step behind, was clear for all to see as they searched for the faintest response. It was a miraculous moment that Sharon and I will never forget. Cindy and Gared loved her . . . they adored her. And for once Jessie actually responded—her ear-to-ear grin literally split her face in two.

All the important people in Jessie's past were there too. Fran, her old pre-school teacher, Gerry who'd babysat her, and her big sister, Jo—they'd all been there through thick and thin. Jessie had also melted the hearts of DADHC staff who'd disrupted their weekends to be there, and even her old school in Newcastle, Lakeside, had sent her a card, the teachers unable to forget a special child who'd fleetingly touched their souls.

I took my guitar out and Jessie bent over and cocked her

head, as if to hear better the first strums. After a few bars she straightened and gently swayed and abruptly stopped, listening again, and then swayed again like a reed in a hesitant breeze showing us all that music could still move her to dance.

Cindy cried and Sharon cried as baby photographs of Jessie's early days in China were passed around. But it was Gared who cried the most. When he helped Jessie eat her birthday cake, when he picked her up and she smiled and when he told stories about a moment when Jessie had shown him—in her way—a love reciprocated.

It was a celebration of her life and Jessie's uncharacteristic serenity catapaulted everyone's spirits sky-high. We were all blessed that day.

As we swept Jessie up to take her home for the rest of the weekend, a blood-orange setting sun lunged through eucalypts with warmth and optimism. Back at home it didn't matter that Jessie got upset over her nappy being changed or having her teeth cleaned; it didn't matter that she might wake up in the middle of the night and scream the house down; nothing mattered. We once again had energy to give. Jessie had the best possible care and Bi Bi could thrive now too.

Later in the evening, relaxing on the back porch contemplating the peace and joy of the day, I took Sharon's hand and squeezed. 'Today was a perfect day,' I said.

'A perfect day,' Sharon agreed and, as she turned to face me, love shimmered in her eyes like Carribean treasure on the ocean floor.

I'll let you into a secret. Despite my often-mentioned optimism in the preceding chapters, the truth is most of the time I was convinced we would never make it; that we'd all be casualties as the world reacted too little and too late to our plight. But

I underestimated Jessie's power. I'm sure now Jessie is special, an 'old soul' as Sharon calls her. Had she stayed in China she most certainly would have been abandoned. It takes my fancy that she was smuggled out by those whose hearts she'd touched, even though they suspected there was something terribly wrong. And now, in Australia, she had four different groups caring for her. Nobody manages that.

It also takes my fancy that, having been dealt bitterly unfair cards, Jessie's destiny is to expose all she meets to the power of selfless love through her purity. If you'd met her you'd know what I mean. At first it seems she has nothing to give, but when you love her all the same, as curiously you must, you realise the power of her gift. It is the warmest sensation imaginable. Everyone loves Jessie, there are no exceptions. *We* didn't prevail, *she* did. No-one can say 'no' to Jessie in the end.

On her seventh birthday Jessie's power was there for all to see in Cindy's backyard where her extensive family of carers, administrators and family friends gathered around her in concentric circles. I'm sure an alien mind, on the outside looking in, would have had no doubt where the source of this blissful power lay.

It was a day when the red threads gathered many of those Jessie was destined to meet in one place and one time. And it didn't matter they could see clearly what was in store . . .

To everything—turn, turn, turn
There is a season—turn, turn, turn
And a time for every purpose, under heaven
A time to be born, a time to die . . .
A time to laugh, a time to weep . . .
A time to dance, a time to mourn . . .

But for now there was still time—for ourselves, for Cindy and Gared—to live in the moment and seize the day, just as the tiny child in a Michelin Man outfit had taught us.